CAPTURE LIFE

Write a Memoir

How to Write A Life Story
Five Techniques to Make It Shine
How to Print and Publish the Story

NIKKI HANNA

Write!
Nikki Hanna

Published by Patina Publishing
727 S. Norfolk Avenue
Tulsa, Oklahoma 74120
neqhanna@sbcglobal.net
www.nikkihanna.com

Copyright © 2016 by Nikki Hanna

ISBN: 978-0-9978141-0-1 (print)
ISBN: 978-0-9978141-1-8 (electronic)

Manufactured in The United States of America

Cover Design: JP Jones, jp@paige1media.com
Photography: Steven Michaels, Tulsa, Oklahoma

ACKNOWLEDGMENTS

Thanks to Melanie Corbin, Lhonda Harris, Tom Bush, and Wayne Kruse for their contributions; to Toni Ellis, Nan McDowell, and Terri Walker for support and encouragement; to Donna Parsons for advice and for championing me so enthusiastically, and to my grandchildren for believing their GoGo is somehow cosmically important.

TABLE OF CONTENTS

MECHANICS OF CREATING A MEMOIR

PUBLISHING A MEMOIR

13. PUBLISHING—THE PROCESS - 171

14. MARKETING AND DISTRIBUTION - 185

INTRODUCTION

Life is transient. Unless a life story is captured, at some point it is lost forever. This suggests a sense of urgency about chronicling it. Yet people delay recording stories because they believe there is more of life to come and time to document it later. **Maybe there is, and maybe not. Life is tenuous. Look around.**

Others don't believe their life is important or interesting enough to write about. They are mistaken. A life story doesn't have to be a universally popular book that appeals to the masses to be significant. There is an audience for every memoir. This book reveals how to discover and describe the essence of a person and the wonder of the world in which they lived. It shows how to do that in a way that people will want to read about that life. **Every life is remarkable and worthy of preservation.**

Some people don't document their life story because they believe they can't write. You don't have to be a writer, nor should you aspire to create a literary marvel. Just tell your story in your own words and in your own way. (Mentally writing to your greatest champion frees your mind so your personality shows up in the story.) Those who know you will recognize your "voice" and appreciate the way you said things because it sounds like you. That means more to readers than a professional writing job.

This book supports novice writers by introducing simple techniques that nourish writing skills and by showing them how to discover a personal, expressive voice. This approach proves that: **Everyone can write.**

While writing and self-publishing my memoirs, I learned how to make a book happen. The process was fulfilling but frustrating. Mistakes were costly, and hard-learned lessons embarrassing. I wrote this book so others could benefit from what I learned.

The focus here is on telling a life story through the printed word. There are other suitable methods. Videos and recordings communicate images and sounds not possible through writing. Such remembrances deliver unparalleled graphic details and liberal doses of visual and audio features. Every medium has its place, each making its own unique contribution to portraying a life. That said, let me make a case for the written word lest it get lost in the stampede toward technological solutions. There is something special about the printed book—that tangible by-product of the written word that can be touched and felt, placed on a shelf or a coffee table, put down and picked back up again, or handed to a loved one. A person can flip pages, gaze at pictures, and linger over robust stories. Embellished with old photos and rich with writer narrative, there is nothing like a book.

> A friend of mine made several videos of conversations with his grandmother, put them on disks, and gave them to family members. It was a wonderful gift, no doubt, but he could tell by talking to relatives that they hadn't listened to it, or at least not all of it. The young are vulnerable to many distractions, and older people struggle with electronic forms.

Perhaps people won't read a book either, but it is not somewhere in a cloud, and it doesn't require equipment to access it. How many of us have tapes from old recorders that have deteriorated or we can't find a machine on which to play them? A book is tangible and accessible, serving as an enduring reminder of the stories within. Its presence is inviting—tempting even. It flirts and coaxes. When choosing a path to capturing life stories, consider the value of the written word.

A broad spectrum of approaches to producing a written memoir, with huge variances in intensity of effort, are available to the writer. At one end is the simple, expedient approach of just getting stories on paper and out there for friends and family. The other end of the spectrum involves writing for a broader audience. This requires acquiring the knowledge and expertise to write professionally, to produce a book, and to market it.

For most memoir writers, the less intensive approach is a better fit. But, wherever your project fits along this continuum, know that there is no right or wrong way to produce a life story. The important thing is that life is captured and shared.

> I wrote two memoirs in order to keep the page count to a reasonable level while still getting out all I wanted to share. (No one wants to read a 500-page memoir.) Also, the audiences for these books were different. The first one, *Out of Iowa—Into Oklahoma* was written for family. (It is referenced frequently in this book to illustrate and emphasize lessons learned while creating it.)

> The second memoir, *Red Heels and Smokin'*, included juicy details left out of the first one. Girlfriends were the audience. These spunky women encouraged me to be bold. (I must warn any man tempted to read *Red Heels* that the narrative will take him to a level of confusion he has never before experienced.) I produced both memoirs in book form because I aspired to be a writer. You do not have to do that.

A wonderful story is possible without the person writing it being "a writer" and without producing "a book." Tell your story in your voice, on your level, and in whatever form you choose. Shape something crazy beautiful, something uniquely yours. The important thing is to capture life stories while you still can. Apply the suggestions herein to the extent they work for you. Where they don't, be audacious about doing your own thing.

Once you've captured your life or someone else's, grandchildren, future descendants, and others will discover a sense of their heritage and benefit from the legacy of your creation. They may never experience the place where their ancestor grew up, but they will know that place. They may never meet the person whose stories you told, but they will know that person. They will not have experienced the times that person lived in, but they will know that history. They will know all this because you captured life.

Through writing, the past connects with the future and generations link together in a common thread. Capture life, write a memoir, and share a story. It will live forever, and you will have given the gift of legacy.

> *A man in awe of a fascinating journal he wrote years ago said, "If I had known it was that interesting, I would have written more."*

People Are Made of Memories.

When it comes to memoir, it is not important that you have the perfect book. It is just important that you have one.

When my memoir was completed, I experienced an incredible sense of relief from knowing I would not die with my story still in me.

I was a lot of fun in high school. So I wrote about that. Next I wrote about old ladies on vacation. Surprisingly, the stories were different in content but similar in substance.

Writing memoir required a life review, which revealed patterns (themes) in my life that explained choices. Examining the past from a seasoned perspective, I understood motivations behind behaviors and reasons for the paths I took.

Once I took a close look at my past, I realized how much I mattered, and I became determined to remain relevant in the future, regardless of how old I got or what happened.

Contemplating myself as a young child while writing my memoir, I fell in love with that child and the adult she became.

Nikki Hanna

– I –

HOW TO WRITE

A MEMOIR

You may say: "I can't write."
The truth is: Everyone can write.

Chapter 1

SETTING THE STAGE

Capturing a life story is a noble and reverent task. What is more important than a person's life? A memoir honors that life—that unique, meaningful, touching history of a life lived. This book provides a roadmap that will put anyone on the path to translating life into a story so compelling that people will want to read it. The big news is that anyone can write a memoir, and that is the most important message in this book.

YOU CAN DO IT: With knowledge, time, motivation, and reasonable expectations, you can memorialize a life, yours or someone else's. You don't have to build a Cadillac. A shiny Kia will do nicely. **You are never going to have the perfect book. The important thing is that you have one.**

My restless grandson fidgeted while eagerly observing my struggle to assemble a toy. "YOU can do it," his squeaky little voice said with conviction. This was not so much an expression of confidence as one of desperation, but his emphasis on the "you" motivated me. And I succeeded.

YOU can do this. You can write about life. Read on and learn how.

VISION: It is important to understand why you are writing a memoir. This will keep you going when challenges invade the process. Whatever the reasons, define them. Express them in goals. Honor them throughout the story-development process. This assures they are realized in the end product. **Keep your objectives always at the forefront.**

Maybe you write because someone asked you to or because you don't want to die with your story still in you. Your goal might be to honor your family, delight elderly relatives, share wisdom, inspire future generations, build family pride, create a record of family history, or all of these things. In the introduction to my first memoir, *Out of Iowa—Into Oklahoma,* I summarized my reasons for writing it.

With the encouragement of my daughter I decided to write this book. She said, "Do it for my kids. I want them to know where they came from and what it was like for you. I want them to know what you know." This was a compelling call to action and just the nudge I needed to retrace my early years, reflect on how they influenced the rest of my life, and record those recollections for future generations.

I am "Out of Iowa" and in a sense so are my grandchildren and any future descendants. They may never see Iowa, but they will know Iowa because I told my story. It is a good thing to know. Iowa is a wonderful place to grow up and a great place to be from. It is a part of me and of them. (*Out of Iowa—Into Oklahoma*)

APPROACH: When teaching memoir classes, I'm often asked: What is the difference between memoir and biography? The lines are blurred, but in general, biography is a factual, comprehensive, chronological account of a person's life. It includes considerable research and detail and is often written by someone other than the person whose life is being chronicled. Memoir is typically written by the person whose story is being told. It is story-like and encompasses only certain aspects of a person's life, those that reveal the person's essence. Just telling about your life is not a story. The following chapters show how to turn a person's history into a compelling story.

Everyone has their own unique objectives for the process of creating memoir and the end product. To accommodate a broad spectrum of objectives and approaches, information in this book is presented on two levels:

Level I: Producing a book or booklet printed in small quantities and distributed to family and friends.

Level II: Producing a commercial book to be published, marketed to a larger audience, and sold through book distribution channels.

HINT: If you choose Level II, the most important action you can take is to join a writers' group.

Whichever method is embraced, readers will find resourceful information herein to guide them through the processes—a roadmap for writing and producing a life story in whatever form meets their objectives. Producing a book is an ambitious project. If you are not so inclined, consider applying the information provided here to journaling, writing short stories, or making notes. These are legacies in their own right.

PERSPECTIVE: Producing a memoir can be overwhelming. If this book leaves you feeling as if you've been hit by a tsunami wave of information, think about the syllabus handed out on the first day of a school semester. Remember how you thought you couldn't possibly do all those assignments. However, when spread over the course of a four-month semester, they were less intimidating and quite doable.

Writing a book is like that. It's intimidating at first blush, but by breaking the process down into segments and spreading the work over time, it is achievable. Many steps are done once to build a base and never have to be done again. Don't let details and numerous action steps derail you from the memoir you aspire to create. Look down the road a year from now and consider all you will have accomplished. Then imagine what you can do in another year. You might be so impressed that you become some kind of crazy and write another book.

Take whatever time is needed to produce the memoir. Find comfort in knowing what you've recorded in drafts is preserved, even if the memoir is not finished. Although on a steep learning curve, you get to determine the timeframes. Take breaks, set an easy pace, and enjoy the process of creating.

The Urgency of Interviews: A caveat to this suggested casual timeframe is: **Pursue interviews with urgency.** You can develop stories later, but having a person-to-person conversation may not be possible down the road, especially if the subjects in the memoir are older people. Put interviews at the top of your agenda. Take a *seize the moment* approach. (Interviewing techniques are revealed in *Chapter 4 - Getting Started.*)

Writing and shaping what you write into a viable work takes time, maybe years. Don't miss the opportunity to uncover the priceless gems that interviews expose—stories and perspectives someone has never revealed before. You may know many facts about a person's life, but the feelings surrounding those facts and the words used to express them in interviews are the jewels of memoir.

> Car time is ideal for getting people to talk. A friend of mine planned to take her elderly mother on a road trip to visit relatives. She intended to probe for information from her mother and the relatives they visited. The day before they were to leave, her mother died. The story will still get written, no doubt, but as is often the case, some enchanting details will not be included.

One more note. The stories of many other people are intrinsically embedded in your story. Embrace this fact, and capture the experiences of others. Diane Keaton wrote her memoirs in *Then Again* with emphasis on her mother's rich treasure of journals. She created a memoir within a memoir, sort of. **No one's story is about just one life.**

> **HINT: When gathering information from older people, ask about their parents, grandparents and other ancestors. Delve deeply into this history. Most of those stories have already been lost. Include what is discovered in your own story. The relevance may be more profound than you realize. What they did brought you to where you are today.**

TIMEFRAME: How long will it take to write a memoir? However long you want it to take. I asked an author how long it took to write his book. He said five years. Another seasoned author I know knocks one out every six months. It's possible to churn and churn and never let go of one. Although it is a challenge to know when a book is "cooked," at some point, you need to cut it off and get it out.

> After working over a year on my memoir, *Out of Iowa—Into Oklahoma*, I was encouraged by a writing class instructor to stop churning and send it to print. I took his advice and regretted it. More polish would have made it better. However, this is a never-ending reality.

Eager to share, you might be tempted, as I was, to release the book prematurely.

> **HINT: Avoid the temptation to rush a book out. If you are dying to share what you've written, give a draft copy or sections of the book to people you trust. Ask for their input. Be sure to retrieve the drafts so they don't float around for years or be discovered in someone's attic someday. As the book evolves, earlier drafts will embarrass you. (This is a sign of progress. You wouldn't want the opposite reaction.)**

Unless you've written a book before, you are going to experience a steep learning curve. Allow time to incorporate acquired knowledge into the book and to produce a memoir that will shine for generations. But remember, it doesn't have to be a professional book. It just needs to reflect a life lived—its lessons, adventures, intriguing details, and the conspicuous expressions and quaint subtleties that made the person unique—their essence.

It took over a year to write *Out of Iowa—Into Oklahoma.* I was retired with time to invest. It would have taken many times that if I had been working. During this time, I went to seminars, read books, did research online, and took computer and writing classes. All that accumulated knowledge was factored into the book. Sometimes I wrote all day and into the night. Occasionally, I took breaks from the intensity of it.

> **HINT: Periodically put the manuscript away for a while. A fresh perspective will emerge and inspire considerable polish.**

Invest whatever time and effort fits your situation and allow yourself to enjoy the process.

Writing a life story is a magical endeavor. Consider this: There are only 26 letters in the alphabet. From them, you can create a 100,000-word, 300-page memoir. Mind-blowing. And that, my dear readers, is the universe showing off. Let me show you how—

Chapter 2

THE REWARDS OF MEMOIR

Producing a memoir is no little thing. It's a lot of work, but the rewards are abundant. The most important outcomes you, as the writer, will treasure include: a fresh perspective on your history, a profound sense of purpose, an intense awareness of achievement, and a sincere feeling of gratefulness. Ah, that's some mighty fine stuff.

PURPOSE: Why write memoir? The memoir-writing process is a creative, introspective, and cathartic experience. Even more important is the influence the end product has on the writer and others. Memoirs are generally tremendously inspiring. The first time I read a memoir as a young woman, I was so influenced by it that I wrote about it years later in my own memoir, *Out of Iowa—Into Oklahoma*.

. . . I read Bette Davis's autobiography. She faced tough times in her early career fighting the contract studio system in Hollywood, going through divorces, suffering abuse, and being financially devastated with children to support. Yet she persevered and rallied over and over.

Her world and experiences were so foreign to me that I was mesmerized by them and how she coped with them. Although I can't say I'm a big fan of Bette, I admired her strength and fortitude, which were especially fascinating because my life had been so cushy.

My Iowa world consisted of stability and intense support systems. No woman would be left to her own devices in that world. I had never observed women with gumption. I saw strong women, but they got things done mostly through patience, persistence, and in many cases, the finesse of manipulation. Bette had moxie, faced problems head on, bucked the system, and took no crap.

After my divorce, when my world turned crazy, I often thought about her desperate struggles and how she ultimately prevailed. It was my only frame of reference for dealing with chaotic change and severe challenges as an independent woman with limited resources and new and burdensome responsibilities. I drew on her experiences for inspiration and hope during that dark interlude and during other difficult times throughout my life. (*Out of Iowa—Into Oklahoma*)

Another person's experiences, once shared through memoir, can profoundly influence someone else's life, as Bette's affected mine. The compliments I most value about my memoirs are from people who said my story inspired them in some way.

A memoir is a gift that flows down through generations, one that paints a picture of a life with all its joys and tragedies. Not only is that life memorialized, but wisdom is shared and legacy created. Any one of these outcomes alone is no small thing. Together they have the potential to transform, or at least to fascinate.

> I sat at the feet of an elderly uncle as he captivated me with stories about World War II. He fought in three major battles in the Pacific. It was unusual for a soldier to be in all three battles and especially exceptional that he survived them. How did this happen?
>
> Confusion over his common name caused him to be shipped home by mistake. When the error was discovered, he was sent back to the Pacific. But instead of being returned to his original unit, he was sent to the next major battle.
>
> After mentioning this in passing to his relatives, I learned they were unaware of this extraordinary tale.
>
> My uncle was soon gone, and I realized then the urgency of capturing a person's

story. If I had not uncovered that history when I did, it would have been lost forever.

HINT: When writing about someone who has died, there are ways to fill in the blanks. Ron J. Jackson, Jr.'s book, *Joe*, about a slave who survived the Alamo, is an example of how to tell a story through research of the world in which the person lived. The history of slaves is difficult to trace, but Jackson brilliantly turns blanks into intriguing details in this book.

Stories of dramatic historical events are fascinating. Others are more subtle but just as worthy. While writing my memoir, I regurgitated information— uncensored, no holds barred—onto paper in the first draft. Then I took portions out that I deemed unworthy of the final book and placed them in an *outtakes file*. My daughter read it and pleaded with me to put some of these outtakes back in.

As a result, I reluctantly reinstated stories about chickens on the farm in Iowa. Yes, chickens. To me experiences around chickens were trivial. To her they were quaint, amusing novelties. She contended that one day they would be fascinating to her urban children. "Mom, my kids will probably never encounter free-range chickens. I want them to know about that."

What is ordinary to you now will be extraordinary to someone years from now. Here is a sample from several chicken stories in *Out of Iowa—Into Oklahoma.* These were stories I was prepared to throw away—stories that time will embellish with surprise and fascination.

Chickens ran free on the farm . . . In modern terms you could say they were free-range chickens. Everyone constantly tiptoed around chicken poop, which was all over the place. We went barefoot all summer. When we stepped in poop, it squished up between our toes, which sent us scampering for the water pump.

Of all the animals on the farm, chickens captivated us kids most. They were accessible. With little effort a child could catch one and carry it around *or whatever.* There was a lot of *whatever* going on.

To small children, chickens were at the lowest end of the farm pecking order with us just one rung up. The other animals could get the better of us, but chickens, well, they were fair game, except for a couple of roosters who made it clear where we really stood in the farmyard order of things.

The roosters were mean and intimidating. They chased us when we were small, wings spread to make them appear larger, necks outstretched, beaks forward. My brother and I declared war on them one day. We put on layers of clothes so they couldn't peck us, took up a garden hoe and a rake, and went rooster fighting.

After a brief episode of rooster war, we believed we had won. In retrospect, evidence suggests otherwise. I imagine Mom looking out of the farmhouse kitchen window observing her children warriors hightailing it for the front porch with a raging rooster on their heels—garden tools abandoned in the dust. . . . As we got older, the pecking order shifted and we looked at a threatening, mean-spirited rooster with considerable arrogance. *Really? You want to do this?*

Our hometown sponsored a pet parade as a community event. We had a couple of dogs and barn cats. With four brothers, these real pets were spoken for, so I had to decide between a chicken and a baby pig. I chose the chicken, which was significantly quieter and somewhat easier to control than a squealing, twisting boar—at least so I thought.

Mom and I went to the chicken house to pick out the hen to be my pet for the day. An old one was selected because we thought she would be mellow. We overlooked the fact that she was excessively grumpy. Mom rigged up a basket for me to carry her in, dressed me in a bonnet and calico dress, and I carried "the little red hen" in the pet parade.

Not being a real pet, the hen was not fond of the idea. Additionally, she was hungry. Chickens are always hungry. As I struggled to load her into the basket, she spotted a mole on my neck, decided it was something to eat, and pecked it off. I bled. Determined to be in the parade with my brothers, I overlooked that crisis and somehow wrangled her into the basket and kept her there long enough to get down the street. This was in spite of her obvious and legitimate concerns about the proximity of several hyped-up bird dogs straining on their leashes.

After the parade, Mom wrestled her into a box in the trunk of the car. This was a good time, I thought, to suggest we eat her. Mom made it clear that having her for supper was not going to happen. My pet was an egg-laying hen, and a wanton brother with grand hunting delusions and a BB gun had already murdered one of her compadres. Having her for supper was not an option. (*Out of Iowa—Into Oklahoma*)

This is a flavor of a whole chapter of colorful free-range chicken tales ranging from hypnotizing them (really), terrorizing them with BB guns, tossing them off buildings to see if they could fly, and raising and butchering hundreds of them. Though these stories seem ordinary to me, they will, no doubt, be a novelty to my urban grandchildren.

> **HINT: If you think your life is not interesting, consider what was ordinary about your life experiences that younger people and your descendants will never experience. Focus in on those.**

REWARDS: Writing your life story, or that of others, is a solitary, introspective experience. You will spend many hours alone at a computer or with a note pad. But you will be enlightened and liberated, probably beyond your wildest dreams. Here's how:

> With adult eyes, you examine yourself as a child, possibly for the first time. The joys and playfulness you discover are relished and the innocence celebrated. Traumas, hardships, and embarrassments are seen in a new light, and deep compassion surfaces. As the fortitude and resilience of that small being are revealed, you fall in love with the child you once were and the adult that child became.

> As you write, the influences of siblings, grandparents, aunts, uncles, teachers, and

others transform from fuzzy memories into revelations of their imprint on the person you became.

Furthermore, you view your parents from an enlightened perspective. After having played that role yourself, you finally comprehend the challenges parenthood entails. You see Mom and Dad as people, a fresh view beyond the narrow one of parenting. Hopefully, you come to realize that, although they were not perfect, they did the best they could with what they had and what they knew.

Although you may never know the demons they faced, traces of their struggles are revealed for the first time as you contemplate their lives. You uncover personal challenges that are the source of their flaws. This fresh interpretation introduces compassion. Viewing their influences on your life with renewed clarity, you may appreciate more the sacrifices made. Perhaps you thank them.

To experience healing enlightenment, expand memories beyond the facts of what happened and enter the realm of feelings. It's not the events, but how people felt about them that make them important. As memories are resurrected, consider the feelings around them.

The last item in a list of Mom's funeral arrangement instructions said, "You kids take care of each other." These few words reflected a lifetime of determined efforts to keep her children connected. How she must have felt when she wrote those haunting words and how my brothers and I felt when we read them is important. This is powerful memoir material and ideal fodder for elaboration.

As the story develops, you will discover themes in your life you didn't know existed—the threads running through it that manifested themselves in behaviors and choices. You will come to understand what makes you tick and why and how you became the person you are today. Through this introspection, the essence of your individuality will be revealed.

Other people will benefit from your biographical journey. My memoirs fascinated siblings and cousins. And the next generations of nieces, nephews, and cousins enjoyed the details of their parents' youths. Some of them even expressed appreciation for the self-indulgent, preachy lessons learned I shared.

Classmates from my generation resurrected their own memories from the escapades and exploits of my youth. And through my book, I re-connected with some of them.

Neighbors and other people in the community where I grew up wanted copies. Young people bought the book for their parents and parents for their children. (Memoirs make great gifts for anniversaries, birthdays, and holidays.) People I'd not heard from in years contacted me after reading it.

> One of the childhood stories I recounted in *Out of Iowa* was about the custom of leaving fancy May Baskets filled with candy on people's front porches on May 1. We yelled "May Basket" and ran like crazy to the car while children burst out of houses or appeared from hiding places to chase us down and kiss us.
>
> On May 1, fifty-some years later, UPS delivered a May Basket to my Oklahoma front porch from a childhood friend in Florida who had recently read the memoir. If I had realized soon enough what was in that package, I would have surely followed tradition and chased down a horrified delivery man and kissed him.

This was not the only unexpected consequence. I noted in the book that my handsome, young personal trainers, Danny and Levi, had tried to kill me, but that they were cute in the process. They wanted copies (probably because I called them cute).

The memoir became popular in surprising circles. My son plays tournament pool, and his buddies at

Owasso's Fishbonz Pool Hall bought copies after asking, "Is Marty in there?"

My therapist, who invested in me by drawing me out of a post-retirement funk, read it and said, "I am reveling in your awesomeness."

To my amazement, readers wanted their books autographed. This introduced some awkwardness initially, but I soon acclimated to the process.

There were numerous positive outcomes from that memoir—the most important one being a curious and unexpected sense of relief and peace. **I knew I would not die with my story still in me.**

DEFINITION OF SUCCESS: As the book evolves and the skills required to produce it acquired, you may begin to think about marketing it. Doing so is probably more complex than imagined and should not be entered into lightly. You'll understand why after reading the rest of this book. In the meantime, it is helpful to ask yourself these questions: Do you want to just capture life and share it with others, or do you aspire to become a professional writer? Is it important to make money by selling a book?

As you become educated on the immense challenges of being financially successful at writing, managing expectations becomes important. Defining success by something other than book sales and financial outcomes tempers the intensity of disappointments that are bound to come.

This is because making money or even recovering the cost of producing a book is a formidable challenge. Pursue your dreams but do this: **Define success simply as creating a book and sharing it with those who are interested. Success is guaranteed at that level. You can do that.** As far as making money on a memoir, let's talk more about that later.

Be courageous in finding your own path to that life story. Brace yourself for penetrating introspection. Be prepared to be overwhelmed and to adjust to the fluid nature of the process. **If you get stuck, remember that a captivating story is about someone trying to get something they want and encountering challenges that keep them from doing so. Look for those scenarios. Research the actions they provoked and the feelings they evoked, and write about them.**

Do these things and you will experience some kind of wonderful from the biographical experience. Share that joy with others, and you will be successful.

Accomplishing all that requires a concerted effort and significant determination. There will be challenges. The most common ones are revealed in the next chapter. Don't allow them to discourage you. **When trials surface and the spirit wavers, remember: YOU can do it.**

Chapter 3

CHALLENGES

There is some risk to introducing the challenges of producing a memoir so early in this book. They could discourage the tentative writer, but being aware of them removes the shock factor. Hurdles will test the spirit at times. With a heads up, new writers are less likely to let adversity deprive them of their goals. So here is your heads up.

> **HINT: When discouraged with the task of producing a memoir, don't focus on what you don't know or what is challenging in the moment. Instead, consider how far you've come, how much you've learned, and what you've accomplished.**

TECHNOLOGY: Technical skill is required to produce a book. This was a curse to me. I spent a fortune on geeks and endured continuous frustrations. Tedious, irritating problems frequently brought me to tears. When the constant aggravation became too draining to endure, I gave up. With my retirement dream of writing out of reach, a vague and chronic emptiness emerged. I felt like a dinosaur. I didn't fit in the world anymore. This was a loss, and I ended up in therapy.

My counselor recommended a peculiar treatment plan: "Get an Apple computer. Sign up for the support package. This gives you access to trainers and project support." That single piece of advice made me an author and changed what I call "my encore years." With my user-friendly Apple *MacBook* laptop, I was back in the game. I could do some stuff.

Determined and hell-bent, I installed an Apple computer, a wireless thingy, and a printer all by myself in just four hours with only nine help desk calls. I was a high-tech momma, let me tell you. One of the calls to the help desk was to report missing cords. The young fellow was silent. After a long and pregnant pause, he finally spoke, "Mrs. Hanna, I-T I-S W-I-R-E-L-E-S-S." I responded, "Okay, thank you," and hung up. (*Out of Iowa—Into Oklahoma*)

Not only did I write books, I designed covers, sales brochures, bookmarks, business cards and a website. One by one and over time each of these found its spot on the agenda, and all were done. This did not happen overnight, but it did take place within a year and a half. Years later, I'm still learning.

This was accomplished only because I could take my laptop to the Apple store, and "the children" who worked there helped me. I refer to them affectionately as "the children," although they were responsible, mature adults. Because they were two generations behind me, I considered them children—sharp, accommodating little geniuses who refused to accept the premise that I was a technological idiot. These kids patiently and determinedly nursed me through the learning required to accomplish my writing goals.

There were traumas. A help desk child asked me if my cookies were activated. I was not going to tolerate trash talk from the Apple children, so I said, "Well, aren't you the little rascal."

I loved the Apple store with all its chaos and pulsating activity. Although such bustle normally irritated me, the store evolved into my happy place. I did amazing things there, which I could not have imagined when I started out. Also, for the first time in years, I felt connected to younger people. I acknowledged them as contributors in my first book and repaid them with advice, encouragement, and interest in their lives. I even helped one of them with a college paper. We got an A.

If you are not a technological genius, you are going to be severely challenged to create a book unless you have someone to support you in the technical area. Don't wait to begin writing to resolve this problem. Go ahead and get started. Write on paper or whatever works, but know that at some point, technical skills are needed to create an electronic file appropriate for printing. If you can't bring yourself to embrace technology on that level, seek a collaborator. You can have a handwritten memoir copied, but it will be expensive (more about that in *Chapter 11 - Printing*).

A Technical Challenge

Here's a feature for you: The MacBook has a little dot at the top of the screen which is a camera. I didn't know this, so it was a shock at one point in the installation process to suddenly see myself pop up on the screen, large as life, in my jammies, hair askew, and no makeup. The angle was not good. It showed my neck, for god's sake, made my nose look big, and the lighting was horrible. Worst of all, there was cleavage, which generated severe panic, the kind that sets off the fight or flight response. I was on the world-wide web with cleavage, looking like a slovenly trollop. . . . Panic stricken, I rushed to the bathroom to fix up in order to appeal to the more discriminating males.

After regrouping, I adjusted the screen for a better angle, softened the lighting, and reported the problem to a help desk child who assured me no one saw it but me. "But I'm all fixed up now," I said. I now have tape over the little dot. I don't trust it. The computer is in the kitchen, and someone might see me loading the dishwasher naked. . . . (*Out of Iowa—Into Oklahoma*)

Computer Backup: I can't think of anything worse than losing an entire book because of a technical failure. Almost every writer has a horror story about losing important work. Have someone help, if you must, but set up a solid backup capability and routinely verify that it is working.

> **HINT: In addition to a backup capability on the computer setup, periodically attach the electronic book file to an email and send it to yourself. This gets it in an internet cloud. (There are other ways to store documents in a cloud, including an application called Dropbox.) Another way to backup is to copy the manuscript file onto a USB flash drive. Also, print the manuscript periodically. It's a good idea to print drafts anyway to proof and edit from hard copy. Keep the latest hard copy in a safe place. I do all of these backups.**

LEGAL ISSUES: This challenge is scary because even if you've done nothing wrong, people can still sue. You may prevail in the end, but the lawsuit has to be dealt with. Every time an instructor in a writing class talked about legal issues, I became so concerned about the consequences that I gave up on publishing my memoirs. Eventually, I decided I didn't want to die with my book still in me because of lawyers. So I got back in the saddle and soldiered on.

HINT: Don't avoid writing about risky topics. (Juicy topics are the ones that hold a fascination for descendants. Remember *Bridges of Madison County?*) Getting them down on paper provides a hedge against senility and gets matters off your chest. Write with abandon. Just don't publish the dicey stuff—yet. Someday, your nemesis may be dead or you'll be poor enough and old enough to publish without risk. More about this later in the discussion of the first draft.

If you verify facts, honor the perspectives of others, keep the story positive, and remain gentle when portraying people, you can most likely dodge legal bullets. **Be cognizant of potential legal implications, but don't let the fear of legal consequences keep you from capturing life.**

While writing my first memoir, I focused on family-oriented subjects, such as my childhood, parenting, aging, relationships, generation gaps, and how the early Iowa years affected the rest of my life. I avoided, or at least danced around, spicy subjects of unfortunate romances, crazy friends making bad decisions, and a career rife with men who interpreted my presence as an invasion of sacred territory. This reduced legal risks for now, but someday I'll publish these things.

They are a reflection of the times and too fascinating not to share.

Changing names and details so no one can tell who people are provides some legal protection. (If you do this, disclose that fact in the introduction.) You can also write a true story as fiction, but if the goal is memoir, you're probably not inclined to want to write fiction—a whole different animal. It is a challenge to hide an identity, and there is always the question of whether the changes are enough to avoid legal consequences. You can never be sure of that.

A publishing attorney can advise you on such matters, or possibly scare the pa-hoot out of you and take your money in the process. Perhaps you simply write your story, be sensible about it, and let the chips fall where they may.

I'm cognizant of legal risks, but I don't let them prevent me from doing the writing I enjoy. Otherwise, I would be back in the therapist's chair. Every person has to decide the level of risk and caution appropriate for their situation.

COPYRIGHTS AND REFERENCES: Another legal category is copyrights. Controversy exists about the use of song titles or lyrics in songs. Some experts say it's okay to use titles and short phrases, but others advise not to use them without a release. Music is usually copyrighted and song writers are particularly protective of their work.

Technically, a release is required from any living person in a photo in your book. Also, photographers and others can own the rights to photos, in which case you must get their permission to use them. You may be required to give the owner credit in the book as well. (Most really old photos are not protected.)

HINT: If a professional photographer takes pictures of you for the back cover of books you write, get a release from him that allows you to use the pictures any way you want, so you can use them on a website, brochure, business card, etc.

Some art, statues, monuments, buildings and other structures are protected. Even if you take a picture of them yourself, you cannot publish it without a release. In a book I'm writing, I am including a picture of a painting. I obtained a release from the painter. However, someone else owns the painting, so to be safe, I'll seek his permission as well.

References: Don't use someone else's published words without giving them credit. If what is quoted is under two sentences, attribute the quote to the person and reference their work. If more than two sentences are quoted, get the author's written permission. If there is a question about whether something should be referenced, look for the source through a search engine, such as Google.

Some written words are used so often that they become "public domain," which means no one can own them. Put words or phrases into a search engine. If they are all over the place without reference, it may be safe to use them. However, some words are trademarked, which means you must have permission to use them if you are doing so to make money.

Some authors use, "Somebody, I'm not sure who, said . . ." when they are unable to find the source of a quote. Many common phrases and statements are impossible to trace.

> **HINT: If you have concerns about whether something is copyrighted, just don't use it. Write your point in a different way and make the reference issue moot. Most writing problems can be resolved by "writing around them."**

UNWILLING KEY PLAYERS: Interest is aroused when news spreads that someone is writing a memoir. There may be people who adamantly don't want to be written about. Amazingly, when these same people are left out of a memoir, they often feel slighted. If someone insists they don't want to be in your book, consider leaving them out. Write around them. This might be an obvious omission readers puzzle over, but it is the person's choice, not yours. If it is crotchety old Aunt Madge, your book probably won't suffer. If it's Dad, well, that's another story.

HINT: If someone vital to the story insists they don't want you writing about them, try this: Show empathy in your portrayal of them and balance the tough issues with delightful, amusing interpretations. Let them read the draft. Invite them to contribute. (This can be incredibly enlightening.) Odds are they will change their mind. If not, brace for the consequences or take them out of the book. (In most cases, if people are dead, you can write about them without legal consequences.)

Others may be overly concerned about what you are doing and try to control what is written. These folks might become your biggest champions if you seek their input and share passages. If they don't come around, know that it's a free country. You can say whatever you like if you stick to the truth and are prepared for the consequences.

EMOTIONAL ROLLER COASTER: One day you'll feel the in-process memoir is a brilliant, hilarious, captivating piece of literature. The next day it's rubbish. You'll vacillate between pride and embarrassment. At times you'll be certain everyone will view the end result as your folly.

You may also feel self-indulgent and uncomfortably self-absorbed at times because the book is all about "me, me, me." You wonder who cares about your life anyway. The solution is to include all your amazing qualities and accomplishments in the first draft. Then, when shaping the book in subsequent drafts, consider what is really relevant to readers. Don't turn them off with a brag fest. And take out as many first person pronouns as possible (I, me, my).

Conversely, writers are often too hard on themselves. This causes a book to take on a negative tone and reflect a victim mentality. Don't ignore mistakes, hurts, and vulnerabilities. They are what make you human. Focus on how you overcame them and moved on. You also may have to struggle with family and relationship issues, just as in real life. Emotions surface, some you didn't expect. Often, the resurrection of old feelings at this stage of life, when maturity influences interpretations, is healing.

There are a multitude of potential emotional distractions and interferences. When the roller coaster takes you to the bottom, take a break. Talk to someone who champions your efforts. My daughter wanted my book to be written, so she kept me going many times. A brother reminded me my life was relevant. A good friend reminded me my writing had promise.

The roller coaster continues after the book is written. As time passes, you view earlier writings with embarrassment. This is good news. It means there is progress. If a freshman effort is not viewed as amateurish when looking back, you are not learning and growing as an author. As much as I love my first writing effort, *Out of Iowa—Into Oklahoma*, it does not embody the craft reflected in subsequent books. That's okay. Everyone must start somewhere. Ride the roller coaster. Enjoy.

AUTHOR TRAUMAS: When writing memoir, traumas surface that spark regrets and raise questions about why you are doing it. Low moments occur when something you wrote hurt someone in a way you had not anticipated, when a publishing requirement is not met, a referencing rule is violated, or errors are discovered after a book is printed. When such traumas strike, acknowledge that there will be ups and downs. Life is like that, and so goes your book.

WRITING CONFIDENCE: The most formidable challenge to creating a memoir is that voice in your head that says: "I can't write." That is so not true. Writing is putting words together. Anyone can do that. In *Chapter 5 - You Can Write,* five techniques provide the writing novice with a framework that unleashes the writing muscle everyone possesses.

HEARTBREAK: Writers are not naturally tough-skinned, but they need to be. Anne Lamott, a best selling author, had twenty-seven bad reviews in a row on one of her books, but she rallied and kept going. Someone will criticize your memoir, but, hey, you wrote something. That's killer. Toughen up. Have confidence. Know this: **You can write**. That is no little thing. The next chapter shows how.

Chapter 4

GETTING STARTED

To get started, just begin writing. Give yourself permission to write an imperfect first draft.

HINT: If you have trouble getting started, try this: Put pen to paper and write about your room as a child—what it looked like and what you did there. Write about decorations, novelties, sounds, smells, fabrics, colors, views, temperatures, dangers, inconveniences, comforts, and your feelings about those things. Don't take your pen off the paper. Write whatever comes to mind. Let the thoughts flow random and free. When done, consider the stories that can be gleaned from this information.

(Not all this detail will end up in the final book. Too much information can derail a story. Bill Bernhardt in his book, *Sizzling Style,* told how he wrote an elaborate courtroom description only to have his editor delete it with the comment, "Everyone knows what a courtroom looks like.")

Apply this exercise to other settings, to events in your life, to relationships, or to hobbies, talents, or interests. Whatever. This will get you started, but there are other activities to be done at this point.

LEARNING: Learning is a forever gift to yourself. What is learned is a possession no one can ever take away. The best way to learn to be a writer is to write, and the way to become a better writer is to write. Reading is also vital. Writers read. Read memoirs. Read "how to" books on writing. Read writers' blogs. Serious memoir writers study fiction and poetry.

> **HINT: Spend time in bookstores and libraries perusing memoirs. Review tables of contents. Examine style, tone, and the flavor of narratives. Read introductions. Note formats and photos. Analyze titles and subtitles. Study marketing techniques on covers.**

You don't have to be a seasoned writer to create a memoir. An amateur effort has its own charm. Be prideful about whatever quirky, delightfully flawed narrative you produce. However, if you aspire to a more polished outcome, embrace "the craft of writing." (Basic craft information is presented in the *Appendix*.) Serious writers study craft and polish their skills for years. Consider taking writing classes. Instructors are usually established authors. These seasoned experts may critique portions of what you write, which is an exceptional opportunity.

Attend writers' conferences. They are rich learning venues. Many are held in interesting locations with good hotel rates, so they provide great travel options.

Join a local writers' group. Such affiliations provide enlightenment and offer collaboration opportunities. Critique groups are often spawned from these organizations. Other writers will encourage and champion you. These groups are well-connected in the writer community and a lucrative source of information on book signings, writer events, vendors for printing and publishing, and how to avoid scams. Search the web to find groups in your area.

Invest in yourself. Learn. And factor all that learning into your book as it evolves over time. Add wave after wave of polish. Each draft will be a giant step forward. While learning, continue interviewing, researching, writing, and rewriting.

TECHNICAL TOOLS: One of the most notable challenges involved in producing a book is the technical component. Technology is also the most amazing blessing. It is essential to printing a book.

Numerous technical requirements are involved in producing a book. Efficiently setting up the text document, organizing it, formatting it, meeting printing standards, and inlining photos are activities that must be done. You'll also need to know how to save, back up, format, print, and transmit files. All this happens through the use of technical tools. It may seem impossible to do all that, but step by step and over time, **YOU can do it.**

Search Engines: Technology is also an invaluable tool for doing research. A search engine like Google gives access to sources of historical details and provides information on punctuation, grammar, spelling, sentence structure, and all manner of writing nuances. Verification of facts, determining sources of references, finding quotes, locating websites, identifying and researching vendors, and a host of other components of the writing process are efficiently achieved through online searches. Learning how to access information this way provides valuable knowledge that has the potential to broaden your world, connect you to others, and embellish your life.

SETTING UP: At some point, the draft must be formatted, but this does not have to be done before writing starts. Just write. Later, what is written can be converted into the proper format. Formatting details are covered in *Chapter 8 - Writing Mechanics.*

The overriding priorities during the early memoir process are interviewing and writing. Don't put them off to learn formatting or anything else. When you are in the mood to write, write. When you have access to people, interview.

SCHEDULES AND TIMELINES: To stay motivated, some writers reserve a couple of hours a day or so many a week for writing. Some set goals, such as a certain number of pages or words per sitting or a chapter a week. Writing at the same time every day can be helpful. Not everyone needs structure, though. Some writers require discipline to keep from writing all day and night. Do what works. Consider deadlines as flexible targets. If they stress you, adjust them.

To facilitate the memoir process, an Action Plan is included in the *Appendix*. Attaching dates to this plan keeps a writer on task, promotes progress, and measures results. Modify the plan to fit goals. The number of steps is intimidating. Don't let them generate pressure. Use the plan to reflect how far you've come as well as what must be done going forward. (If someone asks you why it's taking so long to write your book, show them this Action Plan.)

PLACES TO WRITE: It is helpful to set up a place to write; however, it can be productive to write in different places. Take a laptop to a restaurant, library, or coffee shop. When traveling, writing is a welcome diversion in guest rooms, hotels, airports, cafes, and on planes.

HINT: Carry ear plugs with you. Poor acoustics and intrusive loud music are trendy in restaurants and public places these days, even in coffee shops. Additionally, ear plugs buffer noise from robust revelers, a person whose voice carries like a NASA blast off, or a parent who responds to whining and screaming children with a positive payoff. I love my ear plugs, the best invention since a suitcase with handles.

KEEPING TRACK: One of the challenges of writing memoir is keeping track of enticing writing ideas that pop into the head at random times. No matter how much you commit to remembering them, ten minutes later they are forgotten.

HINT: Carry a note pad or record notes on a phone. Set up a file in which to drop notes or keep a list. As the manuscript develops, work these notes into it.

INTERVIEWING TECHNIQUES: Interviewing people is a critical part of the memoir development process. Never assume a person won't open up. If one is hesitant, ask them to please tell their story before it is gone forever. Keep the interview conversational. Don't tower over the interviewee. Sit on the floor at their feet if you must. Eat with them. If someone gives short, curt answers to questions, take them on road trips to visit elderly friends and relatives whom you can also interview. During car time, ask questions followed by more questions. Probe. For example, a conversation might go like this:

"Mom, who was your best friend in school?"

"Pearl."

"What was Pearl like?"

"She was smart and fun."

"What else?"

"She lived down the road in a rent house. We walked back and forth. When cars passed, the dust choked us. I could run faster than Pearl. I could run faster than anyone in my school."

"Interesting. What did you and Pearl do for fun?"

"We went to church and had slumber parties. We played Monopoly. I always beat her."

"What did you do at slumber parties?"

"Mom made us popcorn with chocolate on it. Her mom rolled our hair with rags to make Shirley Temple curls. Her mom and dad fought a lot, and I didn't like staying there. Her brother got beat up. We hid in the closet with Skeeter. Pearl cried. I didn't. She kept hugging me. Skeeter licked us. I didn't tell Mom."

"Why not?"

"I was afraid she wouldn't let me see Pearl anymore. We were like sisters."

"What did you like most about Pearl?"

"She was my best friend and we shared secrets. I could tell her things. We talked for hours. We played duets on the piano."

"Is there anything you didn't like about her?"

"She was a redheaded spitfire who stole my boyfriends. I really didn't like her sometimes."

"Really? Tell me about it."

"Some other time. I don't want to talk about it."

"Okay. When did you last see Pearl?"

"She got polio and didn't graduate. They moved away. I don't know what happened to her. Some people were in iron lungs, you know."

"How did you feel about that?"

"I missed her, but I didn't cry. I didn't know what to do when she got sick. Mom wouldn't let me visit her because she was afraid of polio. I wondered why Pearl got it and not me. Maybe she got it swimming in the pond with her brothers. I didn't like swimming in ponds. My feet would get stuck in the mud. My teacher got polio. She had one leg smaller than the other and wore a brace. I got a boyfriend, your dad, and got married after graduation. Everyone shivareed us."

"Shivareed?"

"People drove in our driveway honking horns and hollering. They brought food and drinks, and we had a party. We saw the headlights coming down the road and knew we were in for it. Cousin Donnie got drunk, drove his car into a ditch, and got stitches in his head."

Imagine where two or three hours of asking questions could lead. Nuggets like these beg for elaboration. Was the interviewer surprised to learn that her heavyset mother was once the fastest runner in the school? Google: *shivaree* and *polio*. Ask other relatives about them. The interviewer knew not to press when Mom refused to talk about Pearl stealing boyfriends. Later, maybe. Draw out details about the romance with Dad. What other mischief did cousin Donnie get into if he had a habit of driving down both sides of the road at the same time? Even the dusty dirt road is fodder for stories.

Dig deep for descriptive details and how the person felt about them. Feelings are where the rich stories reside, and from them the essence of a person emerges. Jot down notes as soon as you can or use a recorder. Always have questions in mind that will draw the person out.

TONE: The tone of a book is a critical part of the biographical journey. This has to do with how things are said as well as what is included and what is left out. It's important to contemplate how the overall spirit of the book will impact others. Perhaps you don't care and choose to write with wild abandon, but that should be a conscious decision. Most likely you do care, in which case, tone is fundamental.

> It is often said in the publishing industry that to be interesting, a writer must be willing to kill his own grandmother. Another thought is that there are some things you shouldn't write about until your parents are dead.

These statements may be true if you are indiscriminate and insensitive about what you write and how you say it. There are plenty of examples of famous people pressured by publishers to reveal hurtful and embarrassing information in the interest of creating a provocative memoir that sells books. Don't do that.

This doesn't mean it is necessary to leave out the ugly things. Creative writing can often make them colorful, humorous, or at least relatable. Once a writer determines the tone of the book, it governs what is included and the words used to tell the story. **A memoir writer does not have to write about everything. Omission is an okay choice. There is no rule that suggests a memoir must be comprehensive. It's your book. You get to decide what to put in and what to leave out.**

Use this writing opportunity to create an inspirational legacy. Most people did the best they could with what they had and what they knew. Tell about unfortunate incidents compassionately and turn them into lessons learned. Some may be conducive to introducing humor. Or leave them out.

> **HINT: If you hurt someone with words, you hurt everyone around them.**

Define in your mind what you want to accomplish. If you want to make someone pay for making your life miserable, if you need to get things off your chest and vent publicly, or your goal is to assign blame and seek consolation, then the tone will be negative. It's hard to imagine any good coming from that scenario. If those are your objectives, you may want to retain an attorney.

HINT: If it makes you feel better, express such things in the first draft. Get it all out. Be as harsh and bitter as you like. This is good therapy. Just don't publish those words. Soften the edges for the book. Consider the tragedy of people's lives and what caused them to do the things they did. It is healing to take unfortunate events and portray them in clever, sympathetic ways that reveal the essence of a person and the trials they faced. As a result, bitterness fades.

Every person has experienced some degree of abuse at the hands of others. With this ammunition, they can choose to assume a victim role and fill a book with stories of persecution and trials. Or they can choose to be a winner and paint inspirational pictures of life's challenges and how they overcame those harsh realities. And consider this: At some point, no doubt, you were an abuser. People are flawed. People make mistakes. By appreciating the demons others faced, a negative history is portrayed with hope and promise.

An example of this is Frank McCourt's *Angela's Ashes.* He experienced a nightmarish childhood but wrote a compelling, sympathetic memoir. His resilience stands as a tonic for damaged children and as a cathartic remedy for parents who were the casualty of unfortunate circumstances. Jeannette

Walls' memoir, *The Glass Castle,* is another example of a positive approach.

When viewing toxic adults as hurt children—victims of their own difficult pasts—a sense of compassion and empathy is reflected in words used to describe them.

It is highly likely that by writing a memoir you will offend or embarrass someone, whether intending to or not. Bummer. This is particularly unfortunate if the person is someone you care about deeply and who deserves better. Make people feel important and relevant. Consider their perspectives when writing. This mitigates the prospect of hurting them and enriches the book with diverse viewpoints.

HINT: Pretend you are the person you are writing about when you read what you've written. This perspective will guide you into sensitive territory.

There is latitude when putting a spin on a story. Where appropriate, take full accountability for your role in difficult situations rather than focusing all the blame on others. Be compassionate, take the high road, and be gentle with people. Go for an upbeat, hopeful tone.

It's time to get down to the core business of creating a memoir. Let's talk about writing. This is the fun part, the act of creating. Let the fun begin—

Chapter 5

YOU CAN WRITE

ANYONE CAN WRITE: For many, writing a life story is intimidating. The truth is that any reasonably educated person can put words together, one after the other, form sentences that evolve into paragraphs, and shape them into a story. Simply stated: **Those who believe they can't write, can.**

FIVE WRITING TECHNIQUES: Here are five techniques that will make even the most reluctant and timid memoirist a writer:

> 1 - Break It Down
> 2 - Apply Layers
> 3 - Mine Tidbits
> 4 - Discover Defining Moments
> 5 - Expose Rebel Jewels

****

Technique 1
BREAK IT DOWN

Write incrementally. Don't focus on the whole book in the early stages. Doing so is overwhelming. Break it down. Writing short stories and vignettes about episodes in someone's life is less formidable. Write story by story.

> In her book *Bird by Bird* (one of the best books written on how to write), Anne Lamott tells how her brother was struggling with a school assignment to write about birds. His father, a writer, advised him to just take it bird by bird.

A memoir can be written subject by subject, event by event, emotion by emotion, person by person, story by story. Take something—an incident, an emotion, a person, a character flaw, a talent, a time period, a romance, a place, a pet, or whatever—and focus on it. Develop details, embellish, describe, frame, string words together, build phrase after phrase and sentence after sentence. Insert action. Portray emotions. Grow it into a story through description. Paint it with words. Stay with it. Don't leave it alone until it is a robust story. If you get stuck, jump ahead and write the ending. Then return to fill in the rest.

Then take another incident, possibly totally unrelated, and construct it into a short story. Then another, and another. Eventually, you can string these stories together, arrange them logically, link them with transitions, and weave them into a cohesive whole.

HINT: Keep a list of ideas for potential stories as they pop into your mind. Otherwise, you'll forget them.

Write about whatever topic appeals to you in the moment. Follow your gut. Go wherever your mind takes you. Flow with it. Keep building, heaping on details, revealing emotions, and creating a vivid image for the reader. Even life's minor interludes are rich with latent messages. Ferret them out and make them an integral part of the story.

Mom and Dad fretted about polio season. We didn't go to the doctor for much, but when the polio vaccine came out, they hauled us five kids down to the doctor's office pronto.

The early vaccine was in injection form. There were no immunizations back then, and we kids had no clue what was about to befall us. Since Mom and Dad displayed considerable excitement over the vaccine, we were eagerly anticipating our polio shots—that is, until the first one of us got one and all hell broke loose. It was not pretty.

Smallpox shots came out next, a wicked vaccine that left big scars on our arms that are visible to this day. We got them at school where you did not

want to cry, but they really hurt. There was child
chatter about who cried getting their shot. (*Out of
Iowa—Into Oklahoma*)

Anne Lamott has a radiant, descriptive way of
painting pictures with words. Reading her words will
inspire you to be a better writer. Worth observing is
her self-deprecating humor which sympathetically
exposes human flaws (a great tactic for a memoir).
Her use of metaphor and simile (techniques that turn
stories into vivid pictures) is effective. If you read
only one book about writing, read Lamott's, *Bird by
Bird*. (Stephen King's book *On Writing*, and William
Zinsser's *On Writing Well* are also good choices.)

Lamott's book is somewhat intimidating because we
can only hope to be as good as she, but it will make
you a better writer. The queen of metaphor, like
Bonnie Raitt is the queen of slide, Lamott models
expressive, entertaining writing rich with deep,
philosophical messages. She will get you started,
story by story. And you will discover: **You can write**.

✳✳✳✳✳✳✳✳✳✳✳✳✳✳✳✳✳✳✳✳✳✳✳✳✳✳✳✳✳

Technique 2
APPLY LAYERS

Layering is a three-step process that facilitates
writing on a level deeper than mere description.

First, write down a *fact,* an incident in the history of a person.

Next, gather *details* around that fact and describe them.

Then explore the *feelings* people had about all that.

Write with abandon about these things. This is where the magic happens. The result is a story with interest and depth. Here are examples of this approach:

Mom stated that she and Dad were engaged in 1940. This is a *fact.* When pressed for details, she revealed that Dad bought her engagement ring for $10 after working many hours scooping manure and spreading it on the fields of a neighbor's farm to earn the money to pay for it.

This is one of several interesting *details* around that fact. When asked how she felt about getting engaged, she said she was irritated that she and Dad ran into a couple they knew as they left the jewelry store. It disturbed her that the pair would gossip about the engagement.

This reflected her intensely private nature —a *feeling* about the event which was uniquely hers. Most young girls would have excitedly shown off their diamond. Delving into such feelings reveals the essence of a person.

Mom's intense desire for privacy reflected in this engagement ring incident inspired several references in my memoir including this one about her funeral:

Intensely private, Mom always insisted she didn't want any kind of service when she died. So to honor her wishes, we kids, Mom's sister, and a few others skipped a funeral home event and gathered at the gravesite. Brother Kelly performed a short non-service during which he reminded us several times that it was not a service. Afterward, we all complimented him on a fine and touching non-service. . . . (*Out of Iowa—Into Oklahoma*)

Dad's feelings were similarly revealed when I considered his history:

When Dad was a boy, his older brother, whom he idolized, died. This is a *fact*. Interesting *details* around this event were that penicillin had not been discovered yet. A horse kicked his brother in the leg, and an infection developed in the wound. It overtook him. Enduring the torturous death of this young boy was traumatic for the entire family. Research on gangrene and the treatments of the time would reveal what the family went through as this boy's leg rotted away and eventually took his life. That loss wounded Dad deeply. According to his sister, it is the reason he never went to church again.

———————————————

Later, Mom and Dad lost three babies. The scars from these losses became vividly clear when Dad cautioned my brother, who was playing with his toddler, "Don't get too attached to her. You could lose her." This comment is a biographical treasure. It reveals the depth of Dad's *feelings* around his personal losses and the degree to which they shaped him.

Whole chapters, rich with detail and great depth, are waiting to be derived from such information. Apply the process of discovering *facts* and layering on *details* and *feelings*. Intriguing stories will evolve which any novice can mold into a splendid memoir. Do that and you will know: **You can write.**

✳✳✳✳✳✳✳✳✳✳✳✳✳✳✳✳✳✳✳✳✳✳✳✳✳✳✳✳

Technique 3
MINE TIDBITS

Capturing a life story is not about things of biblical proportions. You are not contemplating the world situation or the nature of the universe. Take a minor detail, a tidbit, and grow it into a story. Concentrate on a feeling, a mood, or an incident and write about it in vivid, expansive detail. Let the thoughts flow. Imagine.

Describe depression as a vague emptiness and then portray what that is like. Characterize bliss, how someone found it, and what it meant to that person and others. Write a chapter on cars, clothes, chores, or riding on the running board of a car.

Relationships between living things are rich with opportunities to elaborate. It doesn't have to be a story about Lassie. It can be a fleeting relationship, with or without a deep connection. In my memoir, I described interactions with chickens—an unlikely memoir subject at first blush. (I mean, what is fascinating about chickens?) But this was a topic teeming with abundant details when explored. I've never been "at one" with a chicken, but I have been "at one" with a squirrel.

> Coco lived in a flower pot on my balcony. I communed with her daily. She ate nuts I put out for her while I drank morning coffee. I could write a chapter about Coco, her stretching routine when she exited her nest each morning, her uninhibited begging, her surprise at toast and popcorn entrees, her ungrateful detachment once fed, her interest in gleeful grandchildren pressed up against the glass of the patio door, and her hysterical

confusion when I moved her flower pot a few feet to get it out of the rain.

When I figured out Coco was a she, I worried about baby squirrels scampering on the lawn chairs in the spring with neighborhood cats circling below. The extent to which I would go to protect them was reflected in the peculiar efforts I took to defend Coco's flower pot from the weather. Few squirrels had R-30 value insulation and an umbrella. I could go on and on. There is a story here, not one of epic proportions, but one about a relationship that was a telling reflection of me, a consummate rescuer.

A way to discover things to write about is to focus on key words that describe something that is out of place today. Such words are rich tidbits worthy of attention and elaboration.

Why does anyone spread *manure?* Where did it come from? How and why was it spread? The answer: Fertilizer hadn't been invented yet. What else was unique about farming back then?

Gangrene killed because penicillin had not been discovered yet. *Polio* crippled people, put them in *iron lungs*, and killed them, and no one knew why. *Strep infections* left children with heart damage. *Babies died* because there were no incubators. When introduced, too much oxygen *blinded babies*. Children died from an *overdose of anesthesia* while having tonsils removed. Families lost children to *measles*. (A family I know lost both of their children to measles within ten days of each other.) When asked how many children they had, mothers put their responses in terms of *surviving children.*

Tidbits like these are prominent in your history, and a single word can reveal them. (Considering this, how can you possibly conclude your life is not interesting?) Bring such subjects up when doing interviews and mine the heck out of them. They are golden.

Be all over the words that people throw out when talking about their past—words like homestead, shivarees, the draft, thrashing, crocheting, Mitch Miller, waltzing, Tennessee Ernie Ford, canning peaches, ditto machines, telephone party lines, road ruts, hovering around a radio, and May Baskets. Listen for such words and, when you hear them, dig deep for details.

Everyday activities are worth mining. Life is not all about spellbinding experiences. Trivial events are fascinating. The world people lived in determined their role in it.

HINT: A new reservoir of tidbits is uncovered when older people are asked about their parents, grandparents, and other ancestors. Mine this information like you're digging for diamonds. Those stories are mostly already lost. Salvage all you can.

Not all tidbits are historical. Bring the reader up to date. The present is important. It reflects from where the person came. Paint a picture of the present and do so with bravado. You could say simply: "Now in my sixties, every morning when I awake I'm grateful for another day of independence." Or, you could mine this tidbit and say:

> Every morning when I awake, before I put my feet on the fluffy rug beside my bed, I focus on being grateful for another day of independence. The fluffy rug is there because I'm into feel-good things these days. High heels and tight jeans are no more. In stores I feel fabrics to make certain they pass the feel-good test before taking an item off the rack. My jammies are soft, the bedding high-thread-count Egyptian cotton, and the towels fluffy. The sofa is upholstered in a fabric that feels like flannel.
>
> When I entered my sixties, discomfort for the sake of appearances or propriety fell

by the wayside. Now, I work to soften my world and that of others, physically and mentally. I find myself enamored with soft clothes and comfort food. . . ."

You have just transitioned to another topic where you elaborate on meatloaf and lemon cake, and the morning ceremony of drinking coffee with snow falling outside while you are *not* concerned about the traffic report.

Describe being sixty, seventy, or eighty through a fresh and buoyant perspective that paints a surprisingly sunnier picture than young readers expect. A portrayal that counters pre-conceived notions about old people and introduces a new model for aging means the young are less likely to dread their own futures. This is a rare and precious gift. If an objective for writing your life story is to inspire the younger generation, this will do it.

This does not mean a memoir writer should put a rosy spin on everything. Unpleasant topics need not be avoided. It is possible to write about personal losses by demonstrating stalwart strength and perseverance. Soften deteriorating health with satiric humor and courageous endurance and acceptance. Vulnerabilities can reflect both frailty and resilience. Use words to spark positive thoughts.

A friend of mine described his father's life this way: "He showed me how to live, and then he showed me how to die." It is possible to show the young how to age with flair and how it is possible to find bliss at any age. Such a message has power. This is a way to make life matter —to add purpose to senior years.

Search for vivid words interviewees use, and then dig deep to describe the temperament and emotions of the person expressing them. Don't stop when you think you're done. Keep going. Put word after word, phrase after phrase, and sentence after sentence, and know that: **You can write.**

****

Technique 4
DISCOVER DEFINING MOMENTS

Look for behaviors in a person's past that they stopped doing and for new behaviors they suddenly took on. Behind these shifts in behavior are defining moments. These gem-like, life-changing events plead to be preserved in narrative. Ask people you are writing about (yourself included) what shook them up —what changed everything and why.

A defining moment often lurks behind a *hook*. Hooks are expressions people often repeat that provide a clue about how they view the world. A *hook* is usually derived from an experience that made such an impression on an individual that they carried the message from it throughout life. In the person's mind, the *hook* is a universal truth, and maybe it is. More detail on hooks is included in *Chapter 7 - The Polish, The Shine.*

Another way to discover defining moments is to ask an interviewee if they could live one experience in their life over again, excluding the obvious ones of marriage and birth of babies, what would it be.

> An elderly man, with a sly grin and a twinkle in his eye, answered this question with: "I can't tell you." That said a lot, and the response was so him. I didn't stop the questioning there, though, and soon he was talking about hunting wildcats in Oregon and getting paid to do it.

Defining moments are often driven by dreams. What dream inspired this man to move from Iowa to Oregon? What gave him the courage to chase that dream? How did he find that unusual job? A fascinating story resides behind these facts.

> On my father's side, two brothers decided years ago to move from Iowa to Oklahoma after the land rush. One of them started making coffins, which evolved into a successful furniture business in Cushing, Oklahoma. The other returned to Iowa saying, "I'd rather

die farming in Iowa than live trying to
farm in Oklahoma."

This comment suggests an intriguing defining
moment. Elaborate on such details, and you will
know: **You can write.**

****

Technique 5
EXPOSE REBEL JEWELS

Everyone has incidents in their history where they
broke away from the mainstream and did the
unconventional. (If not, that in itself is a story.) The
result of this rebel act might be glory days or
miserable consequences. Often people are ashamed of
devastating failures, but those failures are powerful
biographical jewels replete with lessons learned and
evidence of amazing growth. Human frailty and the
struggle to overcome adversity draw readers in.
Conversely, enthralling details of blazing triumphs
are heartwarming. Either way, the audience will relate
to such experiences on some level.

Whether it is your life or someone else's you are
writing about, be brave. Take a peek at bold
departures, hurts, resentments, betrayals, and
unfortunate choices. Convey the pain they reveal, the
festering wounds they left behind, and the lingering
heartaches. Examine the scars.

My man left, and I was devastated. At my regular nail appointment I shared what happened with my manicurist. I cried and she cried. Soon the other manicurists around us and their customers became intrigued by the emotional turmoil and got in on the story and the misery. A tearful, awkward silence gripped us all. It was a sad, sorry situation.

Hairdressers became curious about the drama, and they and their customers were soon swept into the doom and gloom. Every woman in there knew in her soul it could happen to her. A dark, angry cloud came down and swallowed us up. It was as though the life force were being sucked out of us.

As we sank deeper and deeper into the abyss, our only defense was bashing the man and the interloper, which further ravaged the anguished group. The cloud darkened, the gloom deepened, and happy salon chatter turned into melancholy whispers and awkward silence. It was grim.

Later, while sitting in my car as I was leaving, I glanced inside the shop. A lady had just entered and looked around like: *What happened?* It became clear in that moment that, in spite of all the pretty hair and fingernails, I had single handedly brought this normally cheerful, chatty, upbeat place down, down, down into the depths of despair. I mean, Dante could not have done it better.

Given the nature of my man's betrayal, I should have thought: *You aren't leaving, thank god, are you?* Instead, I felt like the victim of a drive-by shooting, and I shared that with everyone. I should have brought champagne and cake, but I brought Dante. Realizing this, a defining moment—one that changed everything—invaded my thoughts. Going forward, I still wrestled with the in-your-face demons of the breakup and the loss, but I determined then and there I was going to save myself and others from the doom and gloom.

I couldn't do it, though. In spite of all that resolve, I just could not pull it off. The wound was too deep, the pain unrelenting, the scar permanent, and that was the end of love as I knew it. . . . (*Out of Iowa—Into Oklahoma*)

―――――――――――――

Once emotions have been laid bare, describe the resilience that fortified the person to rise again and continue on. It is possible to mine rebel jewels without trashing the person involved or anyone else by staying connected with natural emotions rather than bad behaviors. Whether actions are justified or not, emotions always resonate with others. By focusing on them, a penetrating, touching story can be produced that demonstrates that: **You can write.**

(See more examples of these techniques in the Appendix.)

―――――――――――――

THE FIRST DRAFT: These five techniques will get you started writing. Before employing them, though, it helps to understand the purpose of the first draft, which is to extinguish inhibitions and regurgitate memories and emotions.

For the first draft, forget about the audience (you are the audience). Apply your objectives and the five techniques only when they don't interfere with the flow of the draft. This stage is about you and your visceral, unvarnished self. Abandon sensitivities. Vent. Purge. Slop it out. Turn yourself loose. There will be opportunities to polish later. Ann Lamott recommends, "Write a really shitty first draft."

Writing with abandon is fun. Robert Frost said, "Writing freestyle is like playing tennis with the net down." Everyone has a different approach to writing that works for them. For many, becoming a wild, reckless, unchecked scribe during the initial draft stage yields a solid starting point on which to build stories. Let's explore how that works.

The objective of the first draft is to resurrect as many memories as possible as well as the feelings that accompany them. Don't censor yourself. This first draft is yours and yours alone. Write for yourself and no one else. No one need see it but you. Write anything you want any way it comes out—let the thoughts flow. Write for months, if necessary.

Don't worrying about the quality of what is written. You have a license in the first draft stage to deliver inferior, sloppy, randomly incoherent writing.

Consider facts, details, and feelings, but don't be constrained by them. Be self-indulgent. Introduce accomplishments. Brag. Describe your witty nature and sparkling personality and charm. Also, be candid about faults, miscalculations, unfortunate choices, and limitations. Be Raw. Doing so cultivates introspection and self-awareness.

Hard Copy: When you've had enough introspection, guilt, venting, embarrassment, victim mentality gnashing, and shameless self-indulgence, print a hard copy and store it in a safe place. You may destroy it later, but not yet. This is the source document for your book and a form of backup in case there is an electronic failure. It might take you months to write the first draft. You don't want to lose it.

Computerized File: In addition to this printed copy, keep the computerized first draft file. As the book is developed, much of its contents will not be used, but you don't want to lose it, at least not yet.

> **HINT: A universal rule for writers is: Always keep everything you write. Every writer, myself included, has broken this rule, usually with no regrets. Some writing is just garbage— flat out—and much is redundant. And there are passages you can't bear for anyone to see. At some point you can delete them or the entire first draft. But not yet. It is backup.**

WORKING FILE/MANUSCRIPT: Copy the first draft file into another computerized *working file*. This is where the memoir is crafted into a story suitable for sharing with others, which writers call a *manuscript*. Ideally, it's best to keep a memoir page count to under 300 pages in a 6 x 9 page book. If you cannot do that, consider doing two memoirs. A book over 300 pages is intimidating to readers and generally not a good idea.

FRAME OF REFERENCE: At this point, it is important to ponder your *frame of reference*—the core from which you write. **You wrote the first draft for yourself. The manuscript is written for others.** To do this well, consider what you want to accomplish with the memoir. Who is the audience, and what impact do you want to have on them? What do you want readers to experience when they read it? The answers to these questions will facilitate writing and keep your memoir project on track.

> I imagined a devoted, elderly aunt's face lighting up when she read my story. My parents were gone, so I focused on her. She had invested so much in me. I wanted her to see the return.

> I hoped to enhance family connections. I thought about my grandkids reading it as teenagers someday and concluding that Grandma was way cooler than they thought. I wanted the next generation of nieces, nephews, and cousins to discover and appreciate the legacy of ancestors, of my parents, and of theirs.

I sought to poke fun at my flaws and youthful idiot behavior while being shamelessly egocentric about recording hard-earned accomplishments. I wanted to share wisdom and lessons learned, to soften the fall or to inspire the climb of descendants and other young people as they shape their own lives.

I aspired to re-define aging by sharing my voyage through productive and fulfilling "encore years." I wanted to take the fear of aging away from readers.

That's an ambitious list. Maybe you don't have an audience and are doing this just for yourself. That's fine, too. Whatever the motivations, know why you are capturing life and what you hope to accomplish by doing so. While in the working file/manuscript stage, keep this frame of reference in mind. It serves as a compass and, like tone, provides the perspective to determine what is included, what is left out, and how stories are expressed.

OUTTAKES: Set up an electronic file labeled *outtakes*. Assuring good flow requires moving things around in the working file and sometime taking them out entirely. When taking something out, transfer it into the *outtakes file*. Be cautious about throwing writing away (deleting it). You'll be surprised how often those outtakes are brought back into the manuscript or at least referred to again.

When going through the first working draft and deciding what to keep and what to take out, consider what is ordinary to you that would be a novelty to your children, grandchildren, and future generations. Include them in the final copy. Describe them in colorful detail.

For example: The fears, turmoil, intrusion, and family disruptions resulting from the military draft seem ordinary to those who experienced it. But subsequent generations will have no sense of the impact this had on families—unless someone depicts it for them.

Future generations may never gather eggs, bake with lard instead of Crisco, or bake at all. They won't drive a standard shift, hear coffee percolate, take an appliance in for repair, gather around a radio, use a rotary phone, collect green stamps, watch a black-and-white television show with the screen rolling, or create rabbit ears with aluminum foil. They will not know Bob Hope, Johnny Carson, or Joe Cocker. My daughter once asked, "Who's Roy Rogers?" We've all heard of the kid who asked his dad if Paul McCarney was in a band before "Wings." They've never heard of American Bandstand or Soul Train, and they probably know nothing about Vietnam. Are there stories to be framed around such details in your life?

While telling your story, go beyond the facts. Show how these people and events influenced your life or that of others. To do this, it's helpful to understand the components of a memoir. Let's explore them so you can tell about American Bandstand and other details of your life with aplomb and a dash of bravado.

Chapter 6

COMPONENTS OF A MEMOIR

A *foreword* is a short section in the front of a book written by someone other than the author. (Many authors misspell foreword with forword or foreward, which does nothing to impress agents or publishers.) Some confuse *foreword* with *prologue*, which is an introductory section written by the author to set up a literary document. Most memoirs don't contain either one. After the required *publisher's page*, *dedication*, *acknowledgements*, and *table of contents*, readers get frustrated with even more front matter. The call is yours, but consider going straight to the *introduction*.

INTRODUCTION: Here is where the stage is set for chapters to come. Tell why you wrote the book and why someone should read it. Disclose interesting information about the process of writing it. Include qualifiers and disclaimers. (If names or details of events are changed in the book, disclose that here.) Describe the scope of the memoir. **Don't begin the story in the introduction. You are setting the stage, not writing the story.**

> **HINT: Go to a library or bookstore. Review introductions in memoirs. This provides a flavor of what to include and examples of what to do and what not to do.**

Controversy exists in the writer community about whether people read introductions. Long paragraphs and dull narrative, no doubt, discourage readers. Keep the intro under six pages. Break up paragraphs. Add white space. Spice it up. Do everything you can to make the introduction interesting. Don't be afraid to use humor, as in this example:

Today at sixty-something I have a vibrant, purposeful plan for my next thirty years. Although at times I feel that the older I get, the better I was, in reality I am more vigorous than ever. Life has never been better. That is, except for the people living in my attic who sneak down at night to steal slippers, hide reading glasses, disable the TV remote, and eat my last PayDay candy bar. (The Introduction in *Hey, Kids, Watch This—Go BEYOND Aging Well*)

Consider including in the introduction a statement about "the truth." Explain that everyone's perception of it is different, that memories are selective, and that people create their own stories in their minds about what happened. Over time, memories fade, and when people recall events, they reconstruct them. Your story is yours as you see it. Others may see it differently. Everyone filters events through their own reality. (Have you ever heard siblings claim they experienced different parents?) Acknowledging that there are divergent interpretations of the past shows respect for the views of others while defending your own.

TABLE OF CONTENTS: Some experts suggest starting the writing process by creating an outline of the book. This organizes the material and assures cohesiveness and logical flow. A *table of contents* can serve this function as well. Either structural framework helps the writer order incremental, story-by-story accounts into rational sequences. Identifying chapters and arranging them in a logical order is a fluid process —many changes are likely as the book evolves.

> **HINT: Choose words used in the *table of contents* thoughtfully. Make them clever, interesting, and enticing. Readers explore the table to decide if they want to read a memoir. Potential buyers refer to it when making purchasing decisions.**

STRUCTURE: The key to the good overall flow of a book is strategic sequencing. Stringing stories together and organizing them through the framework of an outline or a *table of contents* brings balance to random writings. Arrange them so that the humorous, the intense, and the more mundane but critical parts are interspersed. If a chapter is weak, rework it.

> **HINT: Employing a *narrative arc* (more commonly employed is fiction) has the potential to enhance a memoir. This concept is beyond the scope of this book, but if you Google it, you can explore that prospect.**

Structure the book so it has a beginning, middle and end. Grab the audience with the beginning and wow them with an ending that pulls everything together and sums up the major theme. Fill the middle with enticing details (the middle must not suck) and references to the beginning and to earlier chapters. Connect the parts with transitions. Build to the end.

There is a propensity to present information chronologically in memoir. That makes sense to some extent, but if this approach is done exclusively, the book tends to read like a diary, journal, or genealogy report. Creating chapters based on topics, such as people, locations, events, interests, romances, careers, hobbies, or some other category and running those over whatever timeline applies is more interesting. For example, devote a chapter to grandparents, parenting, a beloved pet, high school, Montana, hiking, or grief. Perhaps you include one on a vacation, a success, a trauma, a family crisis, or some other significant event. Make the chapters story-like.

THE FIRST PARAGRAPH: Nail the first paragraph. Think of an agent who gets a hundred manuscripts a week looking at the book and reading only the first paragraph. Would she be interested enough to keep reading? Would someone picking up the book in an airport gift shop or a bookstore be motivated to buy it after reading the first few sentences? Also, determine the most important message in the book and get that in the first few pages or at least hint at it. Do it in a way that creates curiosity and captivates the reader. Action in the beginning of a book draws readers in.

> **HINT: For an example of action, read the prologue to *Water for Elephants*, by Sara Gruen. Readers may not be inclined to read a book about circuses in the early 1900s, but the prologue grabs them and sucks them in.**

Just as the first few paragraphs of the first chapter should grab the reader and tell, or at least hint at, what the book is about, the first few paragraphs of every chapter should do the same for it.

THE THEME: Everyone's life has several themes. They are revealed in the first draft. A theme is a person's way of being in the world—a frame of reference that runs throughout their life and drives interpretations, choices, and behaviors. The introspective nature of memoir writing affords a perfect opportunity to identify and understand themes in your life and those of your parents, siblings, and others. As you forage through the past, these themes emerge and resonate as dramatic influences.

When you identify the predominant theme of a life and refer to it throughout the book, a common thread is woven from beginning to end. Mention the theme or demonstrate it in the beginning to set the stage, refer to it throughout, and nail it in the last chapter. The theme might be craving excitement and taking risks or a slow and steady nature. It may be a talent for seeing the novelty in things and expressing that through humor. To some people it's all about money and achievement, and to others it is about animals or art. Some folks collect things, others collect people, and some do both. A theme reflects how a person interacts with the world. It defines them.

> I discovered the theme of "rescue" as I developed my memoir. I was a passionate rescuer, which explained the men and careers I chose. Other themes of "having something to prove" and "just trying to matter" also surfaced. (I was a middle child in a large family.) I ran these themes throughout the memoir, which revealed how rescuing, having something to prove, and trying to matter coalesced into a powerful force for achievement and a persistent quest for solutions to problems. These themes are why I wrote this book. Rescue is my game.

FINDING YOUR STYLE: Once the basic organization is established, edit the working draft. Refine and embellish the copy using the *five writing techniques* defined earlier.

Writing a memoir is not creating an academic document. Write like you talk. At the suggestion of a writing class instructor, I took contractions out of my memoir draft to make it more proper and literary. Later, I regretted having done so because the writing didn't sound like me, and I didn't aspire to be *literary*. So I put many of them back in. If this is your first serious writing effort, it may take awhile to find your style, but as you progress, a certain way of saying things will become comfortable. Have the courage to be unique, expressive, quirky, and true to yourself. Be proper or unconventional, whichever suits you.

> I took a novel approach to creating the index in *Out of Iowa—Into Oklahoma*. I naturally posed questions when writing the book, so the index consists of a list of questions with the associated page numbers. From these questions, a reader can find their way around in the book.

> In the back of the book, I also included a bulleted list of lessons learned from my life experiences, many of which were illustrated in the memoir stories. I inserted humor throughout this list to overcome the

increasingly short attention spans of young readers accustomed to obtaining short bursts of information from an electronic device.

You can stray from common practices, but in the final product, it is best not to deviate from basic grammar, punctuation, and sentence construction requirements. To produce a polished memoir, seek out an editor.

That said, let me introduce contradictions. First, it is better to do some things half way than not at all. Writing a memoir is one of those things.

Second, grammarians argue ardently over grammatical and punctuation rules, so getting all that right is an exercise in futility. Don't get in a wad over being perfect. You're not writing a thesis, and rules can be broken. The goal is to communicate, not to get an A.

Third, be brave. Your natural writing style might be quirky and irreverent. The epitome of unsophistication can be zany and goofball enough to generate buzz and make everyone want to read the book. (If you choose to avoid the norm and follow eccentric instincts, write playfully so you don't end up in an intervention.) If being boring is your biggest fear, go ahead and turn your crazy, mad, flamboyant self loose. (Send me a copy.)

THE STORY: Ah, the magic of language—milk this magic for all it's worth. Turn that working draft into a story. Polish, enhance, and arrange the text into a logical sequence. Then print what you've written in hard copy. Working from that, re-consider chapter and story sequence. This is when the *narrative arc* mentioned earlier is created. Hone the manuscript down to less than 300 pages. Move things around for logical placement while focusing on flow and balance. Firm up the *table of contents.* This is much easier to do from hard copy than from a computer screen.

> **HINT: You are going to need hard copies periodically throughout the book development process. Printing a book draft on a home printer is time consuming. A better option is to electronically place print orders online with an office supply store. In a few hours the copy is ready. Or take a USB flash drive into the store. (Have the file printed on both sides of the paper and designate black-and-white printing on standard paper to keep costs down. A 200-page book will cost about $30.)**

Check facts in the draft and verify as much information as possible with others. Qualify memories you are not sure of by stating that this is how you remember them. Perhaps you insert other people's interpretations when they are different from your own. That can be interesting. Your feelings and thoughts may not be someone else's truth. Anticipate the perceptions of others and consider the validity of your memories and theirs. Write a story that is mindful and respectful of others, but don't disregard or sacrifice your perspective. Bottom line, if someone sees things differently, they can write their own book.

PROFOUND MESSAGES: Scripting a story is a rare opportunity to convey meaningful messages to young people. Seek out significant lessons emanating from the lives of others. Emphasize sacrifices and demonstrate how people have invested in the future of those who follow them. Strive to elicit pride among readers who discover details of their predecessors' lives through what you write. Where appropriate, present people as positive role models. Indomitable spirits are a source of inspiration and encouragement. Don't miss the opportunity to reveal profound messages, to spark a sense of heritage, and to suggest a worthy path for readers.

HISTORICAL CONNECTIONS: Look for ways to intersect life's events with historical ones. Portraying experiences this way generates a history lesson. Explore feelings about these events. **It was not so much the cold war that was significant about my generation's childhood, but rather the fear it provoked.**

> I compared my generation's cold war fears (fallout shelters, scary training films about nuclear blasts, and fear of annihilation by the Russians) to the fear of terrorism today. This was a revelation to my children who had no concept of that challenging time.

Every generation has its historical nightmares, wars, and tribulations that provide intriguing story opportunities. The impact of wars on my family was profound. Dad experienced the gnawing apprehension of the draft during World War II. My four brothers did the same a generation later during Vietnam. (I celebrated a brother's hip injury. It kept him out of the war.) To my children these wars and the draft are a vague historical reference. That history takes on more meaning when portrayed in the context of consequences to one's family.

CHARACTER DEVELOPMENT: Develop people into the interesting, complex, vulnerable characters they are. Describe them in detail both from a physical and personality perspective. Make them sympathetic characters so readers relate. Concentrate on the essence of each person—what makes them unique.

For example, a brother portrayed as simply "ornery" might be better described as "intentionally playful and unintentionally a bully." Describe Uncle Hank as Noah-like and sturdy, Aunt Edith as waif-ish and fragile, or a couch potato as someone tending toward inertia. Describe how someone who always wore black looked like three-quarters of a donkey cart when she showed up in a colorful dress. One person called her a piñata and threatened to beat her with a stick. Then expand on those descriptions. Search a thesaurus for unique words to characterize each person.

HINT: A thesaurus is your best friend. When struggling with describing something, plug a word into an online thesaurus and find a better one. (Where possible, avoid using important words twice in a paragraph.) A reviewer complimented me on my vocabulary. It was the thesaurus. Don't overdo it. You are looking for better, more descriptive words, not bigger ones.

Show how people change over time. This is known among writers as a *character arc* (Google it). Readers love observing characters evolve. Even someone becoming damaged and cynical is gripping. Life hurts sometimes. Absorbing story lines, themes, and transitions are what make a book a page-turner.

A writing seminar instructor advised that when using real people in a book, get their written permission unless the names, descriptions, and backgrounds are changed so they are not easily recognizable. I didn't do that. After perusing memoirs in bookstores and libraries, I concluded that other writers didn't do it either. At any rate, by developing characters in as flattering a light as possible without substantially misrepresenting anything, I felt comfortable with including people without asking them to sign releases.

Sticking to facts and being as accurate and truthful as possible, making touchy topics entertaining or heartwarming, and omitting or dealing gently with the ugly stuff reduce the likelihood that someone will take issue with what you write. Cranky old Aunt Hazel might get a kick out of your description of her and the outrageous stories about her if you paint her in the right light. She is probably proud of her contrary disposition. Label her spunky instead of grumpy and zany instead of really, really weird.

HINT: In the case of unsympathetic characters whom you don't want to leave out, say something nice about them followed by a comment, such as: "In some ways she was difficult to be around. In other ways, she was a hoot. I found her entertaining, if I didn't take her too seriously." This make a point while minimizing legal fodder.

If you are concerned about including a living person in the story without their written approval and you don't want to leave them out, consult a publishing attorney. I chose not to let legal fears complicate the process of telling my life story or keep me from realizing my writing dreams. If something legal comes up, I'll deal with it. I suspect that's a remote possibility. Perhaps we get more courageous about such things as we get older. When you are ninety and run out of money or are the last man standing, you can write anything you want (a reason to keep the first draft). In most states, there is no cause of action for slander if a person is dead. There is a perverse synergy to that. It is something to boost the spirit when contemplating living that long. Ain't life grand?

BIASES/JUDGMENTS/OPINIONS: During the uninhibited first draft process when memories flow freely, biases and opinions are reflected in the content. They are valid, personal interpretations of life. **But just because you think something in your head doesn't make it universally true. It is a thought.**

Others have their own thoughts and their own personal truths. To avoid being too opinionated and preachy, remove or soften biases. It's okay to have opinions, but you are not writing this book to sway people to your beliefs, but rather to capture a life story.

It's challenging to share wisdom with future generations without coming across as preachy. Since conveying lessons learned may be one of the reasons you write your story and because your beliefs are an integral part of you, go ahead and include a few opinions and philosophical meanderings in the final manuscript. But soften them and express an appreciation for the divergent opinions of others. This takes the edge off judgment and shows respect for those you are trying to reach. When opinions overwhelm a memoir, credibility is lost. If you want to write a manifesto, do so, but that is not a life story.

Massaging the working draft and shaping it into a book is just getting started. Now that there is some semblance of organization and structure, let's turn it into a manuscript ready to print. Let's polish it up until it shines like a new Corvette.

Chapter 7

THE POLISH, THE SHINE

Polishing is the fun part of memoir writing. Let's steal some shine. Let's make your story sparkle.

RUN-THROUGHS: This is a laborious but exhilarating re-writing process. It is where the magic happens. A valuable tool for the novice writer who thinks he cannot write, the process involves going over a working draft many times, each time with different objectives. This involves building the story in layers and polishing it. Every run-through layers another level of depth and shine onto the manuscript. Each one moves the story forward.

With every pass, the story is rounded out, embellished, and re-organized. The quality of the mechanics (format, sentence structure, punctuation, grammar, and spelling) is improved. By focusing on specific objectives during each pass, the book becomes increasingly robust, more cohesive, and the flow is enhanced. **If you are not a writer, run-throughs will make you one.**

Each run-through involves going over the text from beginning to end with the primary focus on a specific objective as listed below. Two or three compatible run-throughs can be combined into one pass. Some passes go quickly and others are tedious and take a considerable investment of time. All are worthwhile.

RUN-THROUGH OBJECTIVES

- **Develop characters:** Physical attributes, backgrounds, jobs, speech, perspectives, temperaments, quirks, character traits, talents, flaws, vulnerabilities, strengths, hopes, losses, how the person dresses and moves, how they express themselves, how they influence others, and their way of being in the world.

- **Establish growth/change in character(s):** (Google: *character arc*)

- **Add descriptive detail:** Develop scenes, describe settings, cultures, environments, smells, colors, textures, structures, noises, temperatures, terrain, and possessions.

- **Add dialogue and quotes:** Sprinkle these throughout the manuscript. Portray how people express themselves.

- **Relate personal experiences to historical events:** Describe the time and place in which the person lived. Paint a picture of unique historical happenings—the big bang events of the time and minor events with major consequences.

- **Make minor things major:** Mine the tidbits. Build them out. Explore colorful, descriptive ways to paint a picture and add meaning. Target experiences that no longer happen and are foreign to young people. Contrast them with today's world.

- **Organize stories:** Print a hard copy of the draft and rearrange the stories. Massage the table of contents.

- **Create transitions:** Assure a flow from sentence to sentence, paragraph to paragraph, and chapter to chapter.

- **Interject sentiment:** Express spiritual connections, passions, and relationships with people, animals, nature, and the world. Layer on feelings, but avoid words *feel, felt, thought*, etc. (show, don't tell).

- **Show rather than tell:** Replace expository information with dialogue, behaviors, expressions, and action that convey emotions. (Google: *show vs tell*)

- **Eliminate the "I factor":** Remove unnecessary self-indulgent remarks and as many *I's, me's*, and *my's* as possible. (When writing in second person, take out as many *you's*, and *your's* as possible.)

- **Interject humor:** Consider the light side of stories. Keep jokes going by referring to them throughout a chapter or in other places in the book. (Don't overdo.)

- **Tighten up:** Remove unnecessary words and redundant sentences and paragraphs. Don't state the obvious. Target 300 pages or less for the final book.

- **Incorporate a theme throughout:** Introduce it in the first chapter, build it in throughout the memoir, and zap it in the ending. (Don't overdo.)

- **Develop a narrative arc—storyline:** (Google: *narrative arc*)

- **Write in active voice (as opposed to passive voice) where appropriate:** Passive voice is *not* wrong, but writing is generally stronger when active voice is used. (Google: *active vs passive voice*)

- **Enhance writing technique:** Eliminate *has, had,* and *have* where possible. Use *would* and *could* only for situations involving uncertainty. Use *that, which,* and *who* correctly. See *The Craft of Writing* in *Appendix* for more enhancements.

- **Avoid "empty" words:** Writers have a tendency to overuse *some, any, the, that,* and *all.* Eliminate where possible. In the case of *it, they, them, there, this, item, thing,* and *something,* consider substituting a more descriptive word. These words are okay to use, but do so judiciously.

- **Eliminate distracting words:** Don't use unnecessary or redundant adjectives or adverbs. If a word ends in *ly,* consider taking it out. Use words like *very, really, rather,* and *pretty* sparingly, if at all. Rarely are they necessary and they can be trite. Evaluate the value of every word.

- **Enhance and improve sentences:** Go over every sentence and improve it. Consider the structure and the order of sentences in a paragraph. In general, put the strongest sentences at the beginning and ending of a paragraph. Use variations of sentence structure.

- **Look for words or phrases to emphasize:** Italicize, use quotes, or bold for emphasis. (Be economical with use. These can be distracting if used too often.)

- **Enhance format:** Introduce white space. Break up long paragraphs, indent whole paragraphs for emphasis, use bullets, and create lists. Set out dialogue. Don't use tabs to indent (a formatting requirement for electronic books, which is becoming standard). Use spaces or the ruler indent process.

- **Enhance word selection:** Use more interesting, colorful, and descriptive words. Put trite words into an online thesaurus and find better ones. Don't use an important word twice in a paragraph. If you can't think of the perfect word, put a less than perfect one in a thesaurus and see what comes up. Caution: Don't use big words for the sake of using big words.

- **Deepen descriptions:** Add descriptive detail that paints a picture. Embellish and describe something by comparing it to something else. Use metaphors and similes. (Don't overdo.)

- **Repeat elements:** In *Out of Iowa* I used tools in a comedic way to relate completely separate events to each other: Dad used tools to charcoal, Mom used tools to open a bottle of wine, and Grandma used a tot's toy tools to feed him.

- **Check the organization/structure:** Print a hard copy. Review for flow and rhythm. Assure that sequences make sense (strategic sequencing). Look for a beginning, middle, and end in the book and within each chapter. Hone down the page count.

- **Check spelling:** Read word by word and syllable by syllable. Verify spelling of any questionable words.

- **Check punctuation:** Obtain an authoritative source book, such as Strunk and White's *Elements of Style* and use it to assure consistent application of punctuation rules.

- **Check grammar:** Review for subject/verb agreement, proper tense, good sentence structure, and consistency of person.

- **Check for consistency of point of view:** Avoid head-hopping unless doing so strategically. (Google: *point of view*)

- **Read the manuscript fresh:** Let it bake. Put it aside for a week or so and then do another run-through.

- **Read the manuscript out loud:** This will reveal awkward sentence structure. The words should flow smoothly. Seek rhythm while assuring variation of sentence structure.

- **Read the manuscript from a hard copy:** Search for errors.

- **Read the manuscript wearing other hats:** Pretend you are other people. View stories from their perspectives. Consider interjecting more sides of the story.

- **Read the manuscript from the perspective of your harshest critic:** Polish it so it's difficult for that person to effectively challenge anything in it.

- **Read the manuscript for fun:** Did the tone and content reflect your vision and purpose? Did you enjoy it?

- **Repeat any of the above as needed.**

These run-throughs might appear daunting, but going over and over a manuscript is how writing is done. You will be rereading and reworking it many times anyway, and this gives each iteration a purpose. I went through my first memoir over sixty times in the period of a year and a half. That's why it takes so long to write a book. If you could just knock one out, read it through a few times, and publish a great book, you would be a masterful writing genius. Most of us are not that. In fact, no writer does that, except perhaps Stephen King and a few other established writers who have support systems and editing resources most of us don't have.

Think of runs-throughs as massaging the book, enhancing it, giving it life. Relish the creative aspect of each pass. Remarkable progress is made with each one. Marvel at how much the draft improves with each run-through, so much so that it becomes difficult to end the process and go to print. You have learned that one more time will yield a substantially enhanced manuscript.

EFFICIENT WRITING: Several run-throughs are designed to encourage "writing tight." This means using minimum words, no repetitive thoughts, and no sentences or paragraphs that say the same thing only differently. It means avoiding adverbs and not using two or more adjectives together that mean the same thing. It means removing unnecessary words, sentences, and even paragraphs. Be ruthless. Make every word count. The greatest comment I received on a business book I wrote was: "There was not a wasted word in it."

WRITING STRONG: Make every sentence meaningful—each one communicating something interesting, informative, entertaining, or emotionally compelling. Assure that all sentences provide information that contributes to the story.

> **HINT: Use the "find" capability on the text software to efficiently target words throughout the text for possible deletion or replacement (as per *The Craft of Writing* in the *Appendix* of this book). This "find" capability can be your best friend—a vital tool for efficiently enhancing a document.**

ACTIVE VOICE: Write mostly in active voice. Passive voice is appropriate at times, but active voice is generally stronger (Google: *active vs passive voice*). This involves using stronger verbs. Take the words *been, be, being, can, would, could, have, had, was, is,* and *will* out where possible and rewrite using more powerful verbs. Don't say Dad *would start* the fire or a fire *was* started by Dad. Say Dad *started* the fire.(Since memoir is historical and almost always in past tense, it is acceptable to use past tense verbs, *was* and *were*, more frequently than in other genres.)

TRANSITIONS: Once you've done enough run-throughs that the order of things is fairly set and the *table of contents* established, focus on the *transition run-through*. Having good flow is vital to readability and to keeping the reader's attention. However, Sometimes an abrupt shift—a jolt—is used intentionally for dramatic effect.

> **HINT: Text that doesn't flow well or is awkward shows up when reading out loud from hard copy.**

At the end of each chapter, incorporate something that entices the reader to read on to the next one, so he doesn't put the book down. This is done by ending the chapter with a question, a cliff hanger, or by teasing the reader with hints about what's to come. Thematic nuggets are candidates for transitions and for echoing throughout a book. Don't overdo, though.

HUMOR AND EMOTION: Include something for everyone (every age group) in the memoir. Interject humor or emotion throughout. Nothing lifts the spirit like humor, and you can make just about anything humorous. Bring a smile to the reader's face or, conversely, a tear to the eye. Or convey such a strong lesson that it touches the reader in a profound way.

For example, technology is not normally a funny subject. It is frequently annoying. However, irritating topics done lightheartedly and with flair are ripe for generating chuckles. Most readers relate to them.

Love Me Some Technology

I embrace technology because I have to, not because I want to, and I will take whatever medication is required to make that happen. . . .

I watched my two-year-old granddaughter proficiently and intently navigating a multitude of apps on an iPhone in a restaurant and realized the toys stashed in my purse held little fascination for her. The most amazing thing, though, is that it was clear I would never catch up to where she was that day, and she was two. Although anything electronic made me feel like a cat scratching on linoleum, I knew I had to embrace the world of technology. I did so kicking and screaming, with grave trepidation, and a peculiar sense of adventure. . . .

. . . a young technical genius was demonstrating features on my new laptop and asked me to select a song to download. . . . I couldn't think of any, so he suggested Simon and Garfunkel. I said, "I'm way cooler than that. How about Snoop Dog?" I didn't know much about Snoop Dog, except that he was hip. He went around with his pants on the ground, and he and I had a common interest in gardening. I knew this because he rapped about garden tools (you know, hoes), and he had a fascination with grass. . . . Anyway, I made the point that I knew who Snoop Dog was, after which the technical genius and I settled on Jimmy Buffet. . . .

. . . the Apple store children have a special appeal. Nowhere else do young people engage my generation unless they need a co-signer or a low-mileage car. Although young folks are generally a challenge to captivate, it is important we maintain a connection with them. They may not realize it, but they need us for our wisdom, and we need them to put Rod Stewart ringtones on our phones and Grand Canyon screen savers on our computers. When I accidentally take a picture of my feet with my iPhone, they can show me how to get it on Facebook. . . . (*Out of Iowa—Into Oklahoma*)

Conveying humor in everyday events and revealing emotions behind behavior make a book entertaining and personal. These are the qualities that stimulate memories, touch people, and make them laugh or cry. Write in a way that moves them in some way, like the lady who sent a May Basket to my front porch.

HOOKS: Become a master at identifying hooks, which are crisp, colorful, snappy sayings that are easy to recall. Hooks are short, efficient sentences or phrases that carry a big wallop and are intensely meaningful to the person saying them. A *hook* reflects a person's view of the world. For example: If someone frequently says, "Nothing good happens after midnight," you know there are fascinating experiences and a deep awareness behind that statement.

Comments people repeat reveal what they are about. Hooks are anthems, kind of. An outrageous friend of mine often says, "I have issues." And she does. Another says, "It's raining men, hallelujah!" I don't believe it's raining men now that disco is "out" and my thirties are behind me, but she does. Good for her. A man who says, "The plan is that there is no plan," is divulging an important personal perception. A crotchety old fellow responds to situations by saying, "Don't affect me none." He's revealing a coping mechanism that defines him. You have to wonder what experiences cause him to say that—to shut himself off like that.

Hooks reveal vulnerabilities, fortitude, joys, or bold confidence. Seek out the hooks that reflect your view of the world, and when interviewing others, do the same. Then, explore the life experiences that generated them and the consequences they provoked.

CRITIQUES: When the manuscript is in its final stages, run it by others. It is a generous act for a person to read a draft and provide feedback. (Acknowledge them in the book.) Some will never get around to reading it. Most will be encouraging, perhaps too much so. If they are friends or relatives, they are going to love, love, love what you wrote.

Ask them to be brutal. Having a bad day over candid criticism is a small sacrifice for you to make for a better book. Ask specific questions like:

> What did you like most?
> Where can I improve the book?
> Is anything inaccurate?
> Were you confused by anything?
> What needs more development?
> What was the weakest chapter?
> Did anything offend you?

When people give input, don't respond by justifying your position. Accept their advice, thank them, and adopt only the suggestions you deem appropriate. People may give bad advice. If you are studying writing, you may know more than the reviewers. As the author, you have the final say. Use prudent judgement when accepting advice.

HINT: Your best bet for quality critiquing is to join a writers' critique group.

If you thought writing a book was a simple process, this chapter with all its run-throughs has probably changed your mind. Still, through writing a life story, you may discover writing can be a fascinating pastime. At very least, if you commit to the processes presented herein, you will know that: **You can write.**

After the memoir is complete, it becomes apparent the unique, fascinating life you wrote about mattered —more than anyone knew. The life story revealed the person's relevance, celebrated their essence, and gave their life meaning. **Everyone wants to matter. By capturing life, you made a person matter, and as the writer, you mattered.**

To communicate a life story, it must be transformed into a tangible object. This is a different process from writing. Producing a book requires cautious strategy and informed decision-making. There are threats out there in the printing/publishing arena about which you need to know. In spite of these challenges, you are going to have some fun now. Let's talk about how to produce a book.

- II -

MECHANICS
OF CREATING
A MEMOIR

You are never going to have the perfect book.
The important thing is that you have one.

Chapter 8

WRITING MECHANICS

Creative writing processes are supported by the mechanics, which present the written word in a professional, polished manner. Mechanics are tedious and, if not done well, they distract from the story and its messages. To make your memoir sparkle, take time to learn about the mechanics. You'll feel smart and clever once you do. I promise. Your book will shine, and you will, too.

FORMATTING: This involves designing the presentation of a document. It requires mastering a substantial amount of detail. Learning how to format the text of a book is intimidating if you've never done it before, but proficiency produces a valuable skill with many cross applications. Let's get started.

Book Size: Determine the outer measurements of the book—the book's size. This will affect the page setup. There are standard sizes. If you vary from them, it may cost more to print, and it can narrow your printer vendor choices.

Most printers have their own standard sizes, but *5 1/2 x 8 1/2* and *6 x 9* are fairly universal. I used 6 x 9 for all my books, a popular size, especially for memoir and nonfiction books. (Fiction books are often in the smaller size.)

If you're not going to publish and sell the memoir and plan to produce only a few copies for family and friends, consider the standard page size of 8 1/2 x ll. This is discussed in detail in *Chapter 11 - Printing*.

Font: This involves the size of the letters and the style of type. *Letter size* of text typically runs from 9 to 13 points, depending on how friendly you want the readability to be. It also affects the number of pages and the thickness of the book. The size for my memoir, *Out of Iowa—Into Oklahoma*, is 11 points. I used 13 here. (Most memoir writers and readers are older, and they prefer larger print.)

> **HINT: The computer screen does not always accurately represent the print size as it will appear on hard copy. Print a few pages early on to determine if you are satisfied with the letter size.**

When selecting the *style of type*, use a common one. Exotic styles are distracting. Styles that have a curl (serif) on certain letters like the "r" "y" and "a" are friendly because people are conditioned to them. This book is in "Times New Roman" (some curls), a favored style among writers. "Arial" is a popular style with a sleeker type. It has no curl factor and reads easily on a computer screen. "EB Garamond" is a style that allows for more space between lines. Like the *font size*, the *style of type* can affect the number of pages and the thickness of the book.

HINT: When selecting a type style, check out how italics show up. In some, the distinction between regular type and italics is so minor that italics don't stand out, which is why they are used. Arial and EB Garamond are examples of this. (Here's a trick: Change italicized words to Times New Roman, and italics will show up better.)

Spacing: It is possible to make the text easier on the eye by setting the spacing between letters wider. Standard spacing between characters is 0. This document is set at 1 with some variations.

HINT: Historically, the custom was to put two spaces at the end of a sentence. The current trend is to use one space, which I have done here. This is so popular that using two spaces is

distracting to most readers, and it dates the writer. It doesn't take long to get accustomed to using one space. (Double spaces can be identified and fixed by using the computer *find and replace* capability to find two spaces and replace them with one space.)

In addition to spacing between characters, spacing between lines can be varied. The standard setting for between lines is "1" which is what I used here. (The "EB Garamond" style automatically provides extra space between lines.)

Avoid *widows* (single lines at the beginning or end of a page or single words at the end of a paragraph). Also avoid *rivers* (spaces trailing down through the text—the result of right and left justification).

HINT: Don't indent by using the "tab" on the keyboard. Doing so creates problems for the printer. Weird, I know, but this is true. A word-processing expert can demonstrate other methods of indenting.

White Space: The more white space on the page, the friendlier the text. (This is why *EB Garamond* style is popular.) Break up text by incorporating lists and indenting whole paragraphs as I've done here with the "HINTS" and the quotes from *Out of Iowa—Into Oklahoma*. Avoid long paragraphs.

In non-fiction books, a space between paragraphs (as is done here) is acceptable, especially for "how to" books. For fiction, there should be no space between paragraphs and the first line of each paragraph should be indented about five to seven spaces. Most memoirs are formatted this way as well.

Start headings of chapters at least nine line spaces down from the top. This white space helps introduce new segments.

Margins: For a finished book, margins are right and left justified (as opposed to a ragged edge on the right margin, which is preferred when submitting manuscripts to editors, agents, or publishers—along with double spacing). Most printers require one inch margins all around. This allows room for the book's binding.

Experiment with different letter sizes, type styles, letter spacing, line spacing, and margins and note their impact on the number of pages and readability.

Headers and Footers: Put chapter names and numbers in the header of each page. Page numbers can be in the header or the footer. In headers and footers, use a smaller font size than in the text. I used 10 points here. **Chapter title pages and blank pages should not have a header.**

Page Numbers: Odd page numbers are on the right, even ones on the left. The table of contents, indexes, and other sections that are not the main text are often numbered with small Roman numerals. I don't do that. **Blank pages should have no page numbers.**

Chapters: It's common practice to begin all chapters, table of contents, introductions, indexes, and other sections on the odd page number (the right page in an open book). This means the page on the left is often blank or partially blank, depending on where the previous chapter ends. Unless completely blank, this last page of a chapter should contain at least a paragraph, preferably more, to avoid a "widow" look.

> **HINT: Study formatting. Research it in a style book or online (Google: *standard formats*). (Caution: The standard format for submissions to publishers and agents is different from that required to print a book.) Formatting is discussed further in this chapter under *Editing/Proofing*.**

Formatting Support: Formatting is complicated for a novice, but YOU can do it. If you struggle with it and plan to write only one book, just do the writing and have someone else do formatting. If you have an Apple computer, trainers in the store will assist with setting up format. Don't let this or any other mechanical process keep you from your goal of producing a memoir. What you are doing is too important to be derailed by such details.

HINT: To avoid being overwhelmed with learning what is required to produce a book, break it down into timeframes. Each month, focus on a new skill, such as formatting, proofreading, inserting photos, printing, and cover layout. By setting a new learning objective every month or so, you build an impressive skill level over time. During this process you are interviewing, writing, and applying what you learn. Consider where you will be after a year—an expert at many things you can use for other applications. Looking back at how far you've come, you'll be amazed at the progress.

Editing the Format: When it comes to proofing, concentrating on text and format at the same time does not work well. Each distracts from the other, and you will miss things.

HINT: Apply a two-step process and do format proofing separately from proofing of text.

Verify font, type style, and spacing consistency throughout. Ensure that chapter headings and page numbers tie with the table of contents and that page numbers tie with the index. Check headings and footings. Make certain paragraph and page breaks are proper and margins and indentations are consistent. Look for widows and eliminate them.

GRAMMAR: You want to get this right. Some of the most common grammatical mistakes are listed in *The Craft of Writing* in the *Appendix*.

> **HINT: A pocket-sized style book is a handy reference on punctuation and grammar. Strunk and White's *The Elements of Style* or *The Chicago Manual of Style* are considered definitive sources for style. Susan Thurman's *The Only Grammar Book You'll Ever Need* is good as well. Many style questions can also be answered through online sources.**

The quickest way to research grammar questions is through an online search engine like Google. You'll get several authoritative sources on the rules and discussion of controversial grammar issues. Here are examples of questions I looked up through Google, which demonstrate the immense value of this resource:

> Is it "worse-case" or "worst-case" scenario? It is worst, although most people pronounce it worse. (Searched for: *grammar/worse-case scenario*)
>
> How do you write in active voice? (Searched for: *active voice vs passive voice*)
>
> Is "silo effect" in the public domain so it can be used without referencing? Yes, it is. (Searched for: *silo effect*)
>
> Is it proper to use "backward" or "backwards"? It is backwards in England and backward in

America. Either is correct—just be consistent. (Searched for: *grammar/backwards*)

Dad said, "If you come to a fork in the road, take it." Did he make that up or did he get it from someone else? The source was Yogi Berra. (Searched for: *fork in the road*)

HINT: If you can't find an answer to a grammar, punctuation, sentence structure, or spelling question, write around it.

PUNCTUATION: Oddly, there is considerable controversy around punctuation. Some of it is related to trend and some to the fact there are English and American ways of doing things. Use either, but be consistent.

> Determined to be up to date, I asked young people how to use commas these days. One said, "No one uses commas anymore." Another said, "Don't use commas stupid." Another suggested, "Only use a comma where you pause when speaking." And finally, a brilliant strategist offered this novel approach, "Don't use punctuation. Just use smiley faces."

Interesting advice, but if you want to do punctuation properly, don't listen to the children. Go to a bookstore or on Amazon, review books on punctuation, pick a method, and stick to it. I recommend *The Only Grammar Book You'll Ever Need* by Susan Thurman.

SPELLING: Spell Check will not pick up everything. If you say *sour* instead of *soar*, *asses* instead of *assess*, *sweat* instead of *sweet*, *voluptuous* instead of *voluminous*, *tart* instead of *start*, *or mustard* instead of *mustered*, Spell Check is not going to catch it.

> **HINT: To help identify spelling errors, read the text out loud and pronounce words by syllable. Some suggest reading the manuscript backward, which forces you to look at each word as distinct from the meaning of the sentence. This reveals certain types of errors; however, it is a burdensome process which works well only for shorter works. It's impractical for a book. I would worry about a person who has the fortitude to read an entire book backward.**

Your best protection against errors is expert proofing from a fresh set of eyes. Get an editor.

EDITING/PROOFING: "Editing" and "proofing" are often used interchangeably, but technically editing is broader and encompasses rewriting and restructuring. Proofing involves checking grammar, spelling, punctuation, sentence structure, and formatting. No matter how much editing and proofing you do yourself, it is necessary to have someone else proof your work. A fresh set of eyes will spot errors you missed, no matter how proficient you are. If you think you were careful and don't need someone to look at what you wrote, consider this: You have just used 600,000 letters to create an 80,000 word manuscript. What are the odds you executed all that accurately?

Proofreading was the most tedious, challenging, and frustrating part of producing my memoirs, other than technology. I eventually licked the technology issue. I didn't win in the proofing arena. I found errors in my first memoir after it was published. Since I printed a large volume of books, this was a costly mistake that carried with it tremendous disappointment. But I learned two important lessons. Don't order large quantities of books and, if you tweak the manuscript after it's edited, you risk creating errors.

> **HINT: When you change something in the text, proof the paragraph twice, review the one before and after it, and check for any formatting impact the change caused throughout the chapter and the book. Also, assess the impact on the index and table of contents. Sounds burdensome. It is, but you will have mistakes if you don't do that. One change can affect many things.**

In spite of these lessons, I have not acquired the self-discipline to stop tweaking the book after it has been proofed. If there are errors in this text, it is not the editor's fault. Although I've come to realize I'm not painting a Monet, I can't control the urge to make last minute changes. No lessons have quieted this obsession. If I were a child, I would be put in time out.

Editors/proofers find errors in every published book. As frustrating as that is for a writer, the important thing is that the book exists, not that it is perfect. Nevertheless, you want your book to be as polished as possible, so heavy emphasis on editing/proofing is time, effort, and money well spent.

> **HINT: Print a hard copy of drafts periodically and proof from them. Errors are easier to spot on printed paper than on a computer screen. You might highlight every bit of text. The deliberate act of highlighting puts focus on each word. I reviewed a chapter that way and made sixteen changes, half of them blatant errors. Some proofers suggest following each line with a ruler.**

Professional editors might run $1,500 a book. I've been able to hire one for $2 a page. To some authors, this amount of money can make the difference between whether or not they can afford to produce their book. Each author must decide the amount of financial investment to make and the level of professionalism to present. You don't have to pay for proofing. Ask for support from friends, a student, or anyone proficient in English and grammar. A retired school teacher friend has been a valuable resource for me.

Proofing and editing are skills that can be developed. There are books available on the subject and classes that teach proofing skills. No matter your skill level, having someone else proof the manuscript is a must. My editor found 106 errors in my first book and 61 in the second one after I had proofed them over and over.

> **HINT: To reduce the risk of ending up with a large quantity of books with errors, order a small number of copies rather than a high-volume order. You don't want 100 books sitting around with errors in them. Thirty, not so bad.**

Errors are distracting and they influence the perception of the author's proficiency. You may not achieve perfection, but go for the perfect book and do everything you can to realize it. Just don't fret over perfection. The important thing is you created something. Flaws are patina.

Editing Run-Throughs: In the final stages, do proofing/editing run-throughs. Do them over and over until you find no errors. You will find yourself doing a number of them to get to that point, if you can even achieve it. I never have on a book. I have no doubt if I read one of my published books now, I'd find errors.

> **HINT: If you start at the beginning of the book for each editing run-through, you will tire and miss errors in the latter chapters. Start with the last**

chapter for a run-through and work backward. Or start in the middle. Put emphasis on the newest and most complicated chapters.

Approach every editing/proofing run-through with healthy skepticism and the assumption there are errors, and you are going to find them. When you think it is perfect, proof again. You will find it is not.

HINT: Let the book bake for a week or so. Then do several more run-throughs. You will continue to find errors.

Then give it to someone else to proof. Double check any changes you make as a result of their input. When I double check changes I make to correct errors my editor found, I always discover several were overlooked or not executed correctly. Some created formatting, index, or table of contents errors.

Order a bound copy from the printer for a final "proof" before printing. (See Galley Copies, *Chapter 11 - Printing*) Go over it in detail. Review format and text separately. Guess what. You will find errors.

By mastering writing mechanics, formatting, and proofing, you acquire skills with many applications. Let's move on to another useful skill—the insertion of photos into a book. This has many cross applications, and photos are fun. Nothing jazzes up a memoir more than captivating pictures.

Chapter 9

PHOTOS

Photos are the frosting on a memoir. When combined with words, they vividly and faithfully convey a scene or a persona. If you decide to include them, seek out a graphic designer or be prepared for another learning experience. (You are going to be so smart you'll want to write another book.)

INCORPORATING PHOTOS: Inserting photos into a book can be a technological quagmire; however, YOU can do it. I included photos in my memoir with help from Apple trainers. Once you get the hang of it, working with photos is fun. And the cross application of this skill, once mastered, is expansive.

Why are photos such a challenge? They must first be digitally loaded or scanned into a computer's photo application and then inserted into the book. It's a complex process.

- Photos must be sized to available space in the book. To preserve resolution, do this in photo software before moving it to the text.

  HINT: Inserting photos into the text with a *copy and paste* process yields better quality than *dragging* them in.

- The photo will likely require constraining or expanding and cropping.

  HINT: Ideally, people's faces in photos should be at least the size of a dime.

- Other adjustments are often required to make a photo sharper, more saturated, brighter or darker, and a host of other tweaks. The quality of pictures when printed is unpredictable. The galley copy may reveal needed adjustments. (Photoshop or software on most computers can be used to enhance pictures. Some writers use *picmonkey.com* to adjust photos.)

- Printers require photos have 300 DPI resolution. The camera, scanner, and photo software play a role in making this happen. I studied this for months and never did figure it out. Graphic designers, printers, and photographers argue about DPI requirements. So what to do? I persuaded a book printer to print photos "as is," and I'd accept the quality. Later I printed the same book with photos changed to the proper DPI by a professional photographer, and I couldn't tell the difference.

- Photos must be "inlined," which means grouped (hooked onto the text related to them). Otherwise they float all over the place if changes are made to the text.

  HINT: When inlining photos into the text, always place the photo next to or after the discussion of it—never before.

- The installation of captions below photos requires grouping processes, which attach the caption to the picture.

- The cost of printing color pictures generally prohibits their viability for inclusion in books. Fortunately, for a memoir, there is a vintage effect to using black and white photos. Even fuzzy pictures possess a certain vintage vibe that is appropriate for memoir.

  HINT: Grouping photos together on pages separate from the text and inserting them in the center of a book was common practice in the past. With digital printing, it's easy to insert photos next to the text that refers to them.

PHOTO RIGHTS: Technically you should get permission from anyone still living whose picture you include. Also, a photographer or someone else may have rights to a photo, in which case you must get their permission to use it, and they may require you give them credit. For their own legal protection, some printers and publishers ask writers to attest to having releases from photographers and people in photos.

THE MAGIC OF PHOTOS: I included family photos in my first memoir. Although they could be sharper, the book would not be the same without them. This happened because I went to the Apple store for training where young geniuses advised me.

Photos complicate the memoir process, but by learning to include them, you know how to use them in newsletters, greeting cards, invitations, social media sites, and albums. If you designate a week to learn the mechanics of inserting photos, you will become a budding, technological genius. Really.

More important, photographs are a gift to those who receive a memoir. And they gain value with age. Years from now those photos will be quaint treasures —vintage jewels reflecting and embellishing a life story. The memoir would not be the same without them. They are worth the effort.

Consider using an old photo on the front cover. Put a current picture of yourself as the author on the back cover. Let's explore the details of designing and producing a cover.

Chapter 10

PRODUCING A COVER

The cover is all about marketing. Once someone picks up a book or views it online, the cover is what entices them to buy it. The cover should convey what a book is about and clearly articulate the value it holds for the reader.

If you are not planning to sell your book, the cover will not need to reflect a strong marketing influence. If you do intend to sell it, making the cover a marketing marvel is an opportunity not to be missed. There are three parts to a cover, each with its own role in the overall purpose of influencing someone to want to read a book and perhaps pay money to do so:

The front: This sparks interest and articulates what the book is about through artwork, the title, sub-title, and other points.

The spine: This is what most people see when the book is on a shelf. Executing it well is immensely important.

The back: Verbiage here involves marketing, marketing, and marketing, which conveys the compelling qualities of the book. A couple of glowing reviews and a picture of the author with a short bio round out the back cover.

TECHNICALITIES OF COVER DESIGN: You will likely need graphic design support to produce the cover. Additionally, a marketing or public relations resource would be helpful for verbiage.

Freelance graphic designers charge from $250-$1,000 for book covers. Printers often provide cover design support, but publishers or printers may deliver cookie cutter or poor artistic quality, even though they charge a lot. (More about that in *Chapter 11 - Printing* and *Chapter 12 - Publishing—The Industry*) Costs and quality can vary substantially between vendors. Many writers use CreateSpace for cover design services at a reasonable fee (*createspace.com*).

With the right software and a willingness to learn, you can design a cover yourself. There is a significant learning curve to becoming proficient. However, once graphic design expertise is acquired, you can design brochures, bookmarks, stationery, newsletters, invitations, greeting cards, business cards, and a website.

HINT: Apple trainers will show you how to use their graphic design software.

However, amateur efforts often look, well, they look amateur. Your best bet for a professional cover is a freelance graphic designer who specializes in book covers.

HINT: Members of a writers' group in your area can hook you up with an experienced book cover designer.

For memoir, a vintage looking photo on the front cover can be interesting.

HINT: Stock backgrounds and photos for covers can be purchased at online sites, such as *dreamtime.com* and *shutterstock.com*. These stock companies usually offer some stock for free.

Fonts and artwork on the cover need special attention. Designer fonts add a professional touch.

HINT: Book cover fonts like *League Gothic*, *Chunk Five*, *Birra*, *Coda*, *Garamond*, and *Matchbook* are popular choices. You can Google *fonts* to find more options.

The front, back, and spine of a cover are designed on one continuous page in what is called a "layout file." This is separate from the word processing file where the book's text resides. When you are ready to print, you will send two files to the printer: (1) the cover layout file, and (2) the internal text file.

Cover layout margins must extend at least a fourth of an inch outside the bounds of the book to accommodate what printers call *the bleed*. This excess is required because the background color must run past the book's edge. Then, the excess is trimmed off to the book's designated size.

Do the cover in soft-back as opposed to hard-back. Hard covers are much more expensive and require a sleeve, another major design step. Although some people still value hardbacks, most don't want to pay for them, and those who travel prefer the lighter weight and less bulk of a soft-back. The trend is clearly toward soft-back.

Color covers have become standard in the industry. There is little or no difference between the cost of color as opposed to black and white. Colors are tricky. There can be a significant difference between what a color looks like on the computer screen and what color ends up on the printed cover.

HINT: Colors generally appear brighter and lighter on the computer screen than in print.

The only way to guarantee a precise color is to use the standard *Pantone* colors which have code numbers that are industry standard. A local printer can show you a sample color chart of these standard colors. Companies use them to guarantee their logos are always printed in the exact color. You can give these color numbers to some printers and be more certain of the end result, but not all printers will do that. (Many book printers, such as CreateSpace, run a number of different covers at one time, which restricts their capability to tweak the color for one book.)

Consider ways to make the style of the cover consistent with the character and tone of the book. I explored several colors when creating the *Out of Iowa—Into Oklahoma* book cover, and nothing clicked until I tried green. It was not one of my favorite colors, but when I plugged it into the design, I knew immediately that was the color. I tweaked it to the shade of the dark leaves in the fields of corn that cover the Iowa landscape in summer.

FRONT COVER: The front cover is all about conveying what the book is about and creating interest in reading it.

Title: The title of a book is crucial if you publish. My memoir is titled *Out of Iowa*. By adding *Into*

Oklahoma to the title, I doubled the geographical marketing audience.

Words in titles are used by search engines to find books. Readers can search on Amazon and other online services by key words in titles and subtitles. Don't get too excited about this fact. A book can get lost in the shuffle of volumes. For example, I searched for my memoir on Amazon by the key word *Iowa*, and thousands of books showed up. *Oklahoma* yielded thousands more. The odds of a reader finding my memoir in this environment is beyond slim. However, when I searched by book title or my author name, it came right up. There are two lessons here: (1) Key word searches don't mean much. (2) It's important to market a book by title and to brand yourself as the author.

HINT: You might even develop a logo. Some writers use *picmonkey.com* to do so.

Whether you publish or not, the title should generate interest. Think of it as a "hook," something crisp, captivating, memorable, catchy, and easy to remember that draws the reader in. Use this hook on the cover and in the book. It should relate to the theme and/or the primary message. Keep the title short enough to fit on the spine in large print, or at least structure it so the first few words are appropriate for the spine.

Subtitle: A sub-title is not required, but it provides an opportunity to share details on what the book is about, which facilitates keeping the title short. Also, Amazon searches by subtitle.

Other Verbiage: There is room on the front cover for a few other remarks. Use the word "memoir" to identify the genre. A reference to the person and the primary subject of the book reveals whom and what the book is about. Keep marketing in mind when deciding what to include. How can you summarize in a few words what is inside in a way that makes a person want to read the book? For *Out of Iowa—Into Oklahoma,* I articulated the theme on the front cover with these words:

> You can take the girl out of Iowa, but
> You can't take the Iowa out of the girl.

These words reflect what the book is about—growing up in Iowa and how that affected the rest of my life.

The author's name is prominent on the front of the book, usually in all caps and spaced out. The publishing company's name can be there and/or on the spine.

SPINE: The title of the book and the author's last name should be prominent on the spine. Libraries and bookstores file books on shelves by authors' last names. The name of the publishing company may also be included. The spine is what people see if the book is on a bookshelf. The color and an intriguing, crisp title in large, readable letters are what make a book stand out from the rest. The spine encourages shoppers to pull the book out and look at it. Make the spine an attention grabber.

The size of the spine must be calculated at some point while designing the cover. It is determined by the number of pages and the weight of the text paper. A printer can help ascertain spine size, or you can find formulas online by Googling: *book covers/spine formula*. A 200-page book will typically have about a half-inch spine.

BACK COVER: You must lose your sense of modesty and rave about yourself and your book on the back cover. This is marketing. Study books in the bookstore or library for a flavor of how to lay it on in a concise, convincing manner.

Write in third person, as if you are the publisher talking about the book and author. Describe what the reader will get out of the book. Emphasize lessons and entertainment value. Use emotional power words and incorporate hooks.

A picture of you as the author is a nice touch. People like to visualize the person who wrote the book as they are reading it. Put your fear of vanity aside and promote yourself as the author. This makes the reading experience more real. Brand yourself as an author with your name and a professional photo.

To sell a book, you must have a bar code on the back cover. (See *Chapter 12 - Publishing—The Industry*)

REVIEWS—SILENT APPLAUSE: Because the cover is a sales tool, backs often include reviews. They can also be in the first few pages of the book, or both. If you are going to sell the book, you may want to seek reviews, but it is a lot of work and is not required. It is preferable to use reviewers with impressive credentials or titles. Reviews should be limited to two or three sentences.

> **HINT: Try this in lieu of reviews: Ask relatives and friends of the person you are writing about to give short testimonials about the person. Seek out quick-witted jokesters, older folks, perhaps even a small child. These comments on the back cover and/or in the front pages of the book add charm and amusement. Those providing comments feel vested in the book. Ask for permission to edit their comments down to one or two sentences.**

It is a big favor to ask someone to invest the time required to read a book and review it. Reviews add considerable time to the publishing timeframe. You must get drafts to people and wait for them to read it (some will never get it done) and get back to you in a timely manner with comments. Good luck with that. You must then edit them into short review statements and add them to the book. If you don't use a review, some people will feel hurt.

> I didn't solicit reviews for my first memoir. Instead, I fabricated ridiculous ones and disclosed that they were made up and that "Sometimes I do things I shouldn't." Avoid such maverick behavior if you are seeking a publisher, but if you are self-publishing, you call the shots.

Probably nothing is more important about your book than the cover. Few will read it if the cover doesn't appeal to them. Make it so captivating that when you hand it to someone, they are fascinated. That's a big order, but the cover is everything to a book. Even if you are not planning to sell the book, the more professional you make it, the more it is impressive for generations to come. A polished, quality book with a wonderful cover honors the life of the person you wrote about, whether it is you or someone else.

To realize the wow factor on a cover, you must deliver the goods on printing. This requires serious decision-making. Those decisions determine how crazy wonderful the book will be or what disappointments await. Printing brings a book to life. It also thrusts you into a precarious dance with vendors. This requires that you know what you're doing because, in spite of their hype, few printers/publishers have your best interest at heart. Let's explore printing.

Chapter 11

PRINTING

Once the text and cover are developed, it's time to produce the book. This means printing it. To be a savvy book producer, you must nail the printing.

If the book is to be distributed to family, friends, and other direct contacts, simply print it and share it. If you plan to sell it on the open market, you are entering the world of publishing, which introduces complications to printing. Before we get into that, though, let's talk about the basic printing issues that apply to everyone whether they are selling or not.

After months, maybe years, of working on a book, you will wonder if it is ever finished. It's difficult to know when to pull the plug and go to print. Polishing is a never-ending process. With every run-through the book gets better, so it's tempting to keep going. At some point, though, you must cease creating and produce the book. Once that is done, odds are you will have regrets about things you didn't include or something not developed or polished enough.

> **HINT: This is not a catastrophe. Order small quantities at first, even if they cost more per copy. Later, you can make changes in the book's text file, send it to the printer, and the next order by you or a reader will be more polished. This is the beauty of digital printing and print on demand (more about that later).**

Printing is a big component of the cost of producing a book. This book costs $5 to print (includes shipping) at CreateSpace, Amazon's printing subsidiary. So 50 books cost $250. Prices fluctuate significantly between vendors.

GALLEY COPIES (PROOFS): Your first printing of the actual book will be a few sample copies for proofing. This is done once the book is organized, edited, and the cover is designed. These are called *galley copies* in the industry. An online *print on demand* (POD) company like CreateSpace can deliver a few soft-back, bound proofs in about a week for about $5 each. Use one to review every inch of the book yourself (check formatting and text separately) and give copies to anyone you want to review the book. Have your editor take a peek at it. This is the final chance to polish.

After this proofing, collect all proof copies, make changes in the text file, double proof them, and send the printer the corrected file. Most digital printers will accept a revised file without charge. CreateSpace allows multiple re-submissions. In fact, with print on demand (POD), even when you find an error in an already published book, you can send in a new file, and the next book printed will include that fix. (Only when a book is ordered is it printed with POD.)

Once the proofing phase is finished, the book is ready to print for customers. You need to know some things about the industry to get printing right.

INDUSTRY TRENDS: The printing and publishing industries are in unprecedented flux. The internet, digital printing, print on demand, electronic distribution channels, and innovative marketing models are re-shaping the industry. Influence has shifted from publishers and agents to aspiring writers who can now self-publish. They are doing so in droves. This new-found power has introduced significant challenges for writers. Many are being taken advantage of by printing and publishing vendors who play on unrealistic dreams of the naive.

Historically, commercialized publishers screened out writers who were unlikely to generate substantial revenue. Now, those writers can self-publish, so the screening process no longer happens. Books with little chance of commercial success are being published. Most rookie writers don't understand that. They are unaware of the nuances of the craft of writing, and many harbor unrealistic dreams of a best seller. Book production is a minefield for these writers.

When seeking a printer, you will run into companies with complicated business models who seek a piece of the self-publishing pie by playing on writers' dreams. These printers offer an enticing but expensive potpourri of services that complicate production and marketing strategy. They take the writer's money and possibly even the rights to his book. Unless money is no object and you don't care about ownership, be skeptical of deals from those who solicit your business.

HINT: Scammers and opportunists are out there. Don't be fooled by well-known names and the size of an organization. If a company solicits your business, that should be a red flag. (More about this in *Chapter 12 - Publishing—The Industry*)

Companies may register your book in their name and use their logo on the cover. If so, they are not just printing your book. They are publishing it. You are no longer the publisher. This may not be a good thing, depending on who you are dealing with and your goals.

PRINTING METHODS—OFFSET/DIGITAL:

There are two basic methods of printing: *offset* and *digital*. Offset is best when huge quantities are required. Few self-published writers use it. Digital printing has become the standard. It's quick, efficient, and conducive to producing small quantities.

OFFICE SERVICE STORES: FedEx and office supply stores offer digital printing. These companies can produce attractive 8 1/2 x 11 spiral or tape bound books with card stock covers. Another alternative is to three-hole punch the pages and put them in notebooks with clear covers in which a printed page can be inserted as the cover. Orders are placed online, or you can take the text file (in PDF format) on a USB flash drive into the store for printing.

This option is the simplest for a memoir, but it is probably the most expensive. A 280-page book printed front and back will run around $35 per copy. If you need a few copies for family and friends, this might be your best bet.

HINT: Order one copy and proof it before ordering multiple copies.

LOCAL PRINTERS: Some local print shops can print a book, but they may contract out the binding. (Most small shops don't do binding.) This increases costs and delays delivery. If you go this route, consider getting quotes from several printers. Prices can vary greatly. You may pay around $10 per book

—not a bad price for a gift for family and friends. If you sell to others, a profit is unlikely at this cost.

PRINT ON DEMAND (POD) VENDORS: The print on demand business model has emerged as the preferred approach for most writers. This is because of its relationship to another new kid on the block, online book retailers (companies like Amazon).

These new players have propelled both the printing and publishing industries into a state of flux— revolutionizing them by giving writers access to a new and efficient channel to get books to market. POD companies have a seat at the online sales table primarily because they provide printing and fulfillment (packaging and shipping) for these sales.

The problem is that many of these printing companies use the print on demand (POD) label as a pathway to offering add-on services to writers, including publishing and marketing. This may appear to be a good deal at first blush, but—

The POD business model has blurred the lines between printing and publishing. Because of vendor hype, writer ignorance, and the intricacies of the business, many authors using POD vendors believe they are self-publishing when, technically, they are not. (More about that in *Chapter 12 - Publishing—The Industry.*)

Also, a writer may unknowingly limit his future options through exclusive contracts with these companies. The vendor may even persuade an author to unwisely give up the rights to his work.

> **HINT: The name and logo of a traditional publisher on your book is normally not a problem, but beware of other companies that insist on putting their logo on your book. (More about this in *Chapter 12 - Publishing—The Industry.*)**

After surfing the internet for printing services or putting contact information on a public record (copyright, Library of Congress, book registry), brace yourself for an onslaught of marketing solicitations from these companies. Their communications are lush with enticing stories of writers selling lots of books and making lots of money. Don't get sucked in with the hype. Your best bet as a memoir writer is to avoid such offerings and use a reputable print on demand (POD) company to digitally print the book and ship it to you. Then you can gift it to family and friends and sell it directly to your contacts.

> I've realized the best digital prices and quality printing from CreateSpace, a subsidiary of Amazon. I learned about them from writers' blogs, where they were touted as offering the best prices, the most user-friendly processes, and good customer service.

This company guides new writers through the process of printing. Once that is done, it's a small step to placing a book on Amazon and Kindle. Their production services (cover design/editing) are reasonably priced, and the website (*createspace.com*) is loaded with helpful educational information for novice writers.

HINT: Avoid companies that aggressively solicit your business. If you decide to wade into marketing, seek references from seasoned writers before engaging a print vendor.

****

If you don't intend to sell your book, most of the rest of this chapter will not apply to you. It is helpful information, though, because once you reach out to printers, you are going to experience some of the complications of the publishing industry whether they apply to you or not. Knowledge is your friend.

****

POD PRINTING AND FULFILLMENT: The basic concept of print on demand is that with digital printing capability, a book is printed only when someone buys it. This virtually eliminates inventory management. Digital printing quickly produces a single book at a viable cost. It is possible to seamlessly print, sell, and distribute books through CreateSpace, Amazon's digital printing and fulfillment company. Many seasoned writers use this approach. Once you establish the printing of your book at CreateSpace, here's how the Amazon model works:

Amazon posts books online, accepts orders, collects and distributes money, and records sales transactions.

CreateSpace prints, packages, and ships the books to customers. (As the author, you buy your books at a discount directly from CreateSpace.)

Amazon pays CreateSpace its cut for printing and fulfillment, keeps their share, and puts the writer's share of the sale in an account. This money is periodically wire transferred to the author's bank account.

This is an expedient process and is popular among seasoned, self-published authors, including me. Before contracting for services beyond this basic sales, printing, and fulfillment, model, do a benefit/ cost analysis.

If you chose a printer who offers package deals, things get complicated. Some are vanity publishers (defined in *Chapter 12 - Publishing—The Industry*) masquerading as POD companies. They press writers to purchase other services, which are expensive and unlikely to yield a profit for the author. These vendors make money from authors giving it to them, not from book sales. If you have plenty of money and are willing to incur the consequences of this model, one of these companies can make your book a reality with little effort on your part. Just know that their sales projections are suspect. If you care about that, be smart and deal with companies that make money when a book sells. In general, it is best to avoid the following potpourri offerings of services:

Book Production Services: Some of the packaged services these vendors offer include formatting, editing, cover design, and photo insertion. You can spend a lot of money here. Prices are often inflated and quality inconsistent.

If you have no other sources, these services can make your book a reality at a price, but perform a cost/benefit analysis and understand every provision in the contract. Be thoughtful about signing away the rights to your book, the cover, the artwork on the cover, the right to use another printer, or the right to cancel at will.

HINT: Join a writers' organization and discover who the members recommend to perform these functions.

Wholesaler/Retailer Connections: Print companies may urge you to pay them to get your book listed on wholesaler listings like Ingram, Baker & Taylor, and Bertram. They imply that libraries and retail stores like Barnes and Noble will then buy the book. Getting on a listing does not mean retail bookstores, libraries, or anyone else will buy your memoir. They probably won't.

Online Sales Connections: Printing companies may propose you pay them to get your book on an online book sales site. You don't need them to do that, but if you choose to use them, seek a deal where you don't stand to lose a lot of money if sales don't materialize (no large upfront fees). Review contracts carefully. (Details on what to watch out for when procuring this service are listed in *Chapter 13 - Publishing—The Process.*)

Marketing Services: If you plan to sell a book, odds are slim that a printing company's marketing services will be cost effective. Revenue to you is unlikely to offset the cost—a harsh reality, but true.

The memoir genre is a highly competitive niche category, a fact that further narrows the market. In addition, the net profit per book is shockingly small. Books are almost always sold at a discount, often a hefty one. You may price a book at $15, but it sells for $7.99. Check out the prices of books in a bookstore and on Amazon's online site. (On Amazon, discounts don't affect the writer's share. Amazon absorbs the discount.) Once a seller and a print/ fulfillment company take their cuts, there is little left for you. You may sell 250 books, the average sales for a self-published book, and end up with a few hundred dollars. Keep these points in mind when vendor hype promises to make your book a raging success and earn you "lots of money."

Review Services: For a price, some printers also offer to promote books through newsletters, reviewers, review publications, and online promotion vehicles. These are not customized marketing programs, and they are unlikely to spur meaningful sales, especially for a memoir.

When you pay someone to market your book, they get your money up front, so they are guaranteed a profit. You, on the other hand, are unlikely to get your investment back, let alone make anything, because you only get money if the book sells. You take all the risk. They get the sure deal—your money.

This is not how the book business is supposed to work. **Printers should get paid when they print. Agents and publishers should get paid when a book sells.**

HINT: Companies often ask for your email contact list and the names and

addresses of friends and relatives. DON'T GIVE IT TO THEM. These are easy direct sales you can make, and they offer the largest profit margin. Keep them for yourself. Why give those easy sales to someone else? Why give anyone a cut of the revenue from your own sources? Your contacts are a huge portion of the books you can sell. Keep them for yourself.

Don't be lured into deals that are not lucrative. There is a universal truth in this business. **No matter what promises are made or which business model you choose for sales and distribution (major publisher, a print on demand company, an E-books company, online sales, or a combination of these), you, as the author, are the one who drives sales. You are IT.**

Printing for Direct Sales: Direct sales are all up to you, and they yield the highest profit margin. These are sales you make yourself to people with whom you are in direct contact or who buy through your website. It is the optimal sales opportunity. To do direct sales, you need a supply of books in your possession. You pay for printing and the shipping of books to you, but no one else takes a cut. There is no middleman.

Printing books should run about $5 each (including shipping). Sell them through book clubs, your website, or directly to friends, relatives, and other contacts. If you sell one for $15, you realize a nice $10 profit.

HINT: To be able to sell direct, you must not give anyone exclusive rights to print or sell the book. Red flags should go up when you hear the words "rights" or "exclusive" or see them in a contract or an agreement of any kind.

PRINTING THE COVER: The biggest challenge to printing the cover is getting the colors right. What you see on the computer screen may not be what you get when the proof arrives. Also, what you see on the proof may not be what you get with the final product, another reason to order small quantities.

COATINGS/STORAGE: Without a coating on the cover, the color may peel when the cover is bent or when books rub together in shipping. Laminate or UV coatings in glossy or matte are common, with glossy the most popular. Most vendors coat their books. Climate-controlled storage is recommended; however, I've experienced no problems storing books in the garage. And I've hauled them around in the trunk of my car in Oklahoma heat with no consequences.

PRINTING SPECIFICATIONS: Knowledge of common specifications for printing helps a writer communicate with printers. Here are some:

Pages: 200 - 300
Size of book: 6 x 9 or 5 1/2 x 8 1/2
Cover: 10 point weight

Coating: UV or laminate - glossy
Printing: digital
Logo: no printer's logo on the cover

Most writers submit books to printers electronically, usually in PDF format. The text and cover are submitted in separate files:

(1) a layout file for the cover (a graphic design file), and

(2) a text file for the interior content

DELIVERY: Once changes identified from the proof review are implemented, the book is ready to print. You should have it in two weeks.

> **HINT: Order only a few copies at this point. As you did with the proof, give them to friends and an editor to read. Ask them to advise you of any errors. This appears redundant, but even after all the previous editing effort, errors are in there. Fix them and resubmit corrected files before placing a large order for your inventory.**

I ordered 500 offset copies of my first book. Big mistake. I don't recommend using offset printing or ordering a large volume. Several hundred of these books ultimately ended up at a shredding facility because I found errors in them—a tough lesson learned.

In spite of that mistake, receiving printed copies of my first book produced a significant life event. The day the shipment arrived, a large semi pulled up in front of the house. The airbrakes hissed, and I went to the window to discover a semi truck too large to get into the garage area. The driver said, "No problem. I have a fork lift." I had never had anything delivered to me on a fork lift before, so that was a tad traumatizing. As I opened the garage door, he came at me on the fork lift with boxes of books on a wooden pallet.

After he deposited them in the garage, along with the pallet (a pallet in my garage was also a new experience), I stood there alone, staring at the mound of boxes. *Holy cow. This is going to be a problem for my children when I die.*

The experience was overwhelming, but it was also a fabulous defining moment. After cutting open a box, I got my hands on a copy of my first book and said out loud: "I am published. I *am* an author."

Printing creates the book. Publishing is the mechanism for selling it. Even if you don't anticipate selling, the next chapters on publishing include information you need to know about opportunists. You may not be looking for them, but they will be looking for you.

Note: I refer to CreateSpace, Amazon, and Kindle numerous times in this book because that is the channel I use for printing, sales, and distribution. This strategy has worked well for me as well as for most writers I know, and it's the model with which I am most familiar. It is a simple, workable approach. There are other vendors. Each writer must determine his own path.

- III -

PUBLISHING
A MEMOIR

Through memoir, the past connects with
the future, generations link together in a
common thread, and legacy is created.

Chapter 12

PUBLISHING—THE INDUSTRY

The publishing arena is where a book is promoted and sold. Unless you plan to sell your memoir, there is no reason to publish. Print and you're done. If you cross the line into selling a book, you are entering the realm of publishing. There are three basic tracks to publishing:

(1) ***traditional publishers*** (major to mid-sized publishing houses and smaller specialty publishers)

(2) ***vanity and subsidy publishers***

(3) ***self-publishing***

TRADITIONAL PUBLISHERS: Publishing through one of the five major publishing houses is viewed as the golden ring by many writers. Several medium-sized publishers are also prestigious, and many small publishers are reputable. To authors, the qualities that most distinguish a traditional publisher from others are: (1) they do not ask writers for money up front, (2) they have the muscle to get books into large retail bookstores, and (3) they finance the production of books and make money only when a book sells. So they are highly motivated to sell.

There are downsides to the larger, most prestigious publishers. Since they are profit-driven and blockbuster-focused, the prospect of them accepting a memoir from someone who is not famous or an established author is a long shot. If a major publisher should take on a newbie's book, they believe in it, and it is most likely a winner. However, a writer's royalty rate is a paltry 4 to 15% (as opposed to a self-published Amazon plan that pays 70%), and an agent will take a cut of that. (A writer is required to have an agent to buffer interactions with the publisher.) These publishers usually insist that a writer give up the rights to his book. This is a scenario in which the benefits might make it worthwhile to do so. The author is expected to market the book and have a platform (a substantial online following of potential buyers). Building that platform requires intensive effort. In spite of the publisher's promotional support, the author is the primary driver of sales, and that requires substantial time and effort as well.

Smaller traditional publishers are more likely to publish memoirs written by novices.

> **HINT: By joining a writers' group, you'll learn which of the smaller publishers are popular with the group's writers in your genre.**

Advances: Publishers sometimes give advances, but don't get too excited. Contracts normally require writers to give them back if books don't sell. (I've heard authors say they refuse to return advances.) Huge advances are mostly a thing of the past.

Book Production: A traditional publisher will do the cover design, printing, promotion, and distribution. Writers are subjected to mandated rewrites and have little say on the cover, title, release schedule, or price. It can take a year or two to get a book out. (At a writers' conference in 2016, a writer who had sold his book to a major publisher told me it would be out in 2018.)

Major traditional publishers rarely take on new writers. There are many writers and a limited number of buyers. Supply exceeds demand. Also, most memoirs are not commercially viable. A wonderfully intelligent, artful book may not appeal to the masses. Additionally, new writers often have not mastered the craft of writing. Publishers may accept mediocre writing from a famous person and clean it up, but a newbie must demonstrate expertise. In spite of these drawbacks, many authors consider the large traditional publisher model a good gig, if they can get it. Few can.

LITERARY AGENTS: Most of the large and medium-sized traditional publishers and even some smaller ones, require that writers have a literary agent to buffer relations and deal with details. Getting one is a challenge. An agent takes a 15% to 20% cut of the thin percent assigned to writers from book sales. No agent should charge an upfront fee. If they do, they are probably not legitimate and may be tied to a vanity publishing house (more about that later). An agent's income should come from commissions on book sales, not from authors. **Don't give an agent money. (Check agents out at writersbeware.com.)**

> **HINT: An agent recommended by a seasoned author is a good bet (a reason to join a writers' group). Writers often connect with agents at writers' conferences. A writing class taught by a published author might produce agent contacts. Examine acknowledgements sections of books similar to yours for prospects.**

VANITY/SUBSIDY PUBLISHERS: Vanity businesses require that authors front the money to produce a book. This includes the publisher's profit. By getting money upfront, they are guaranteed a profit whether the book sells or not, so they are not incentivized to sell. Authors gets measly royalties on the few sales generated. Subsidy publishers, a variation of vanity publishers, share in contributing the upfront money but generally recoup their investment before the writer recoups his. (Most retail bookstores shun vanity and subsidy books.) Because of industry prejudices, neither vanity nor subsidy companies are likely to label themselves as what they are. Writers must figure it out. The clue is the requirement that the author give them money.

> **HINT: A writer giving a publisher money upfront to produce and sell a book is what distinguishes vanity from traditional publishing where agents and publishers make money when a book sells.**

Experts generally advise serious writers to avoid any publisher who asks for money. However, if money is no object, if you understand the sales and legal consequences, and if you manage your expectations, a vanity company might be a viable option for making your book a reality.

SELF-PUBLISHING: Introduction of the self-publishing model has shifted the publisher's playpen to a writer's wonderland. This model—made possible by online bookstores, electronic books, digital printing, and print on demand—has revolutionized the publishing industry. It gives writers control and generates the most income from each book sold. Approximately 80% of books produced today are published outside of the traditional publishing arena. They are such a blend of vanity and self-publishing that it is impossible to determine how many are actually self-published by authors.

The growth of companies trying to get a piece of the self-publishing pie has produced a sea of choices for authors, and the lines between true self-publishing and vanity publishing have been blurred. Companies often add the POD label to their offerings to imply to unsophisticated writers that if they sign with them they are self-publishing when they are not.

Self-publishing is essentially running a business and this requires knowledge, time, and effort. However, it is inexpensive and a sure way to get a book out while maintaining control of the process. There are many other advantages that come with this model, but problems for writers have emerged.

True self-publishers are referred to as "indies." They are independent. Bonafide self-publishing requires that an author form a publishing company, own the ISBNs for his books, and is listed as the publisher of record on the *Books in Print Register*. The copyright and Library of Congress registrations are also in his name or that of his company. His publishing company is printed on the book (as opposed to another company's logo), and he holds all rights to the book.

The author contracts for cover design, printing, fulfillment (packaging and delivery), and other services. He may even contract to share the proceeds of sales with a print vendor and a book seller, such as

CreateSpace and Amazon. To avoid losing control of contracted processes in these dealings, he avoids exclusive arrangements and makes sure to keep the rights to his book. When a writer allows a company to take ownership of rights and/or gives them an exclusive to provide services, he is no longer a self-publisher by the literal definition.

Whether a book will sell under the self-publishing scenario is questionable. It is tough to sell books, especially memoirs. This is why traditional publishing companies are unlikely to pick up a memoir. It is also the reason so many companies try to get money up front from writers so they can make a profit regardless of sales volume.

Self-publishing is hard work, but it guarantees a book will be published, and it usually gives the writer a higher cut of the revenue. It may actually involve less effort than a writer would expend trying to engage an agent and publisher, and it gets the book to market quicker. The writer might also avoid some abuse. Folks in the publishing industry can be insensitive.

> Author Anne Lamott had a publisher's editor tell her she made the mistake of thinking everything that happened to her was interesting. Ouch!

> Another author's best selling book was finally accepted by a major publisher after sixty rejections by agents and

publishers over a six-year period. During this time she endured numerous criticisms and mandated rewrites.

Such experiences can be avoided through self-publishing. The writer is not repeatedly begging someone to accept his work. When he is ready to publish, he publishes, and he controls the process.

Since getting a traditional publishing company to publish a book is a remote prospect and vanity companies are in disfavor, self-publishing is a hot trend. An understanding of how to make good decisions and how to avoid the pitfalls of the industry are important to succeeding at it.

SCAMMERS/OPPORTUNISTS: Most writers harbor unrealistic dreams of fame and fortune. If you have such grand illusions, a reality check is in order. Scammers and opportunists stand ready to play on those hopes and entice you to part with your money.

It is like the Wild West out there. Don't take steps to publish until you understand how the bottom feeders of this business work. These guys aggressively track down writers. They are manipulators. Many are vanity publishers, some disguised as something else. A few claim to be Christian companies, implying a level of trust they don't deserve.

Scammers make promises they don't keep. Opportunists may keep their promises, but they play on the naiveté of writers in order to take advantage. Neither scammers nor opportunists take risks. In both of these scenarios, the money flows from the writer to them. They make most of their money from writers giving it to them, not from book sales.

Not everyone soliciting a writer's business is a scammer, but even legitimate companies often overstate the value of their services. The problem is that what they offer may not be financially sound and cannot yield the return required to make the writer's investment worthwhile. This is on the writer. He took the deal.

If you use these companies, you will be writing the checks. Here is how they work:

> They ask for your manuscript. Then they notify you that it is remarkable (which is what they tell everyone). Next, they request a substantial amount of money to produce and sell the book. You send them $2,000 to $10,000. They must sell a lot of books for you to recoup your investment, let alone make anything. Can they do that? It's unlikely. Do the math. (You can self-publish a book for around $500.)

> When you complain that the book is not selling, they ask for more money to fund more promotion. Many people give it to them. Don't be one of those people.

In the publishing industry, authors normally must pay for books they want for their own purposes. Writers with vanity/subsidy publishers have already fronted the money to produce their book, and now they must pay to buy them. What is wrong with this picture? A host of other unfortunate outcomes can occur. Some writers even lose the rights to their work.

Run the numbers and watch out for dubious sales projections. Exercise healthy skepticism about programs offered. When confronted with a proposed marketing deal, remember this: Although it is true that earnings are a function of promotion, the key to selling your book is not what someone else does. It is what you do. Don't be a victim. Use due diligence to check out companies and their offers, or better yet, ignore them.

GETTING EDUCATED/INFORMED: Your best protection from these circumstances is education. Read up on publishing and marketing.

> **HINT: When searching for books on publishing, be aware that some are written by those who have a vested interest in a company that prints and markets books. These books are biased. Consider the source of all information.**

Your best source is other authors. After reading books on self-publishing, I recommend these two, both written by seasoned authors:

The Complete Guide to Self-Publishing
by **Marilyn Ross and Sue Collier**
Everything you need to know to write, publish, promote, and sell your own book.

The Essential Guide
to Getting Your Book Published
by **Arielle Eckstut and David Henry Sterry**
How to write it, sell it, and market it . . . successfully!

These are thick, comprehensive books—almost encyclopedic. There are more condensed ones.

> **HINT: Search for "self-publishing" on Amazon's site. Look for books written by authors. Pick a couple that are right for you.**

If your eyes are glazing over from all this information, don't despair. And don't let the complications of the publishing business keep you from realizing writing dreams. It is not necessary to dabble in all of this. Be aware of the pitfalls and narrow your scope to avoid them. The next chapter tells how to do that.

YOUR PROSPECTS: The reality is that the odds of engaging a literary agent or a major to mid-sized publishing house are not good. And under none of the publishing scenarios (traditional, vanity/subsidy, self-publishing) are you likely to experience a substantial income stream. A high-selling book is a long shot.

For unknown authors, the average number of books sold is 250. There are hundreds of thousands of writers in this country. Bowker, the company that registers books, reports that over a million books are published each year. Only about 5% result in significant sales. Most of those are from established authors or famous people.

Glory stories about authors getting rich represent a minuscule portion of the writing population, but they are highly publicized. Stories of self-publishing being a springboard to a major publishing company are exaggerated. Simply stated, it is possible but unlikely your book will be a big seller. If you find this disheartening, consider this:

> Chase your dreams, but be honest about why you write. Don't let industry bluster define those dreams for you or determine the criteria for your success. Consider this measure: **If you write it, share it, and someone enjoys it, you are successful.** With this standard, you are successful when the words flow. You cannot fail.

Most writers don't write to get rich, although they may dream about that and even aspire to it. They write because they love to create. They relish seeing what they write blossom into a beautiful book that is shared. In the case of memoir, they write to reveal a life story to generations to come—to create legacy. For those writers, it's not about the money. It's not about the fame. It's about why they write—the creation, the artistry, the sharing.

Chapter - 13

PUBLISHING—THE PROCESS

True self-publishing requires that a writer form a publishing company. There are many hybrids of publishing models. The one I illustrate here is the one I use, as do many of my writer friends. With this model, the self-publisher is responsible for editing, cover design, layout, printing, shipping, pricing, and determining production and marketing strategy.

Novice self-publishers sometimes make mistakes that complicate the production process and deliver sub-standard books. Shabby writing craft exacerbates this problem. For these reasons, industry prejudices ascribed to self-published books are well earned. If you self-publish, get your game on and do it right. And brace yourself. You're in for a ride.

PUBLISHING STRATEGY: Develop a strategy for turning your manuscript into a book *before* you begin to reach out to printers or publishers. Define goals clearly and don't let hype take you off track.

A viable solution for many writers is using a small traditional publisher. There are many reputable ones. Members of a writers' group can steer you to those who specialize in your genre. To get one interested in your book, it must be a quality product that demonstrates writing craft.

A memoir must have general appeal to a broad audience to entice a traditional publisher. Remember, they make money when the book sells. You must have a viable product. If you are a memoir writer with the objective to share a life story only with people important to you, seek a printer or perhaps even a vanity publisher (if you don't mind shelling out the money). Just make sure you don't get sucked into the hype and taken advantage of. Keep your objectives in sight.

A SIMPLE SOLUTION: As a self-publisher, consider this model:

> (1) Use CreateSpace to print books and to do fulfillment for Amazon and to reformat for an electronic Kindle connection.

(2) Use Amazon to sell printed books and the E-books, record sales, pay CreateSpace their share, and send you your cut.

(3) Develop a website and sell books there by linking it to Amazon.

Using this model, you can avoid many problems novice writers face. If you consider any other model, be vigilant. Some writers successfully use a draft-to-digital company (*draft2digital.com*).

CAUTIONS: Here are points to consider when selecting vendors and negotiating contracts as a self-publisher:

- Recognize that companies seeking first-time writers to give them "a big break" are actually seeking the naive to get them to part with their money.

- Don't give an agent or publishing company money up front to publish a book.

- Know that royalty percentages may be misrepresented and overstated because of complicated and vague formulas.

- Unless signing with a reputable publisher who makes money only when your book sells, be cautious about letting anyone put their logo on your book. Some experts say certain logos prohibit books from being accepted in bookstores and causes them to be shunned by serious reviewers.

- Some experts recommend caution about sending a manuscript to potential agents or publishers. Unless you are dealing with someone who only makes money when your book sells, sending only a couple of chapters might be best. An unscrupulous company can steal your book and sell it overseas where western books are popular, and you will never know. Or, a publisher might steal your idea, have someone rewrite with enough changes that it is no longer yours. Although there are horror stories about these threats, the prospect of either of them materializing for a memoir is slim.

- Reputable companies do not engage in exaggeration to get business. Don't believe glory stories of wealth, fame, and a top-selling book. Success stories are often distorted, and represent a small percentage of writers. Consider the failure rate.

- Be skeptical of paying someone money to get your book in national bookstores through "wholesale distributors." Getting your book listed with wholesalers/distributors does not mean bookstores or libraries will order it. Also, be careful about paying for professional reviews or critique services. Such reviews are unlikely to generate meaningful sales.

- Don't give anyone money to advertise a book unless you satisfy yourself it has the potential to generate enough net cash to you to make the cost worthwhile. In spite of the hype, the likelihood of that is often remote.

- Before signing a contract, perform a financial analysis. Make certain there is the prospect of a viable return on what you invest.

- Publishing attorneys collect sizable fees for answering simple business questions. Fees can be more than the potential risk. Instead of engaging an attorney, consider eliminating the risk by changing strategy.

- It is standard in the industry for a writer to buy his books from the publisher. In the case of the traditional publishing firms, that's okay because you haven't given them money up front to produce the book. With those where you have fronted the money, why should you have to pay for copies?

- Google any potential publisher. Look for lawsuits and Better Business Bureau complaints. Use *writersbeware.com*, a site that reports complaints and scams.

- Understand the consequences of letting anyone else register the copyright, the

Library of Congress Control Number, or the ISBN. (I know self-published writers who let CreateSpace obtain these. I do not.) If someone else does it, they may be listed as the publisher of record, not you. If you intend to be the publisher of record, that may be a problem. Otherwise, it may not, especially if you are dealing with an established, trustworthy, traditional publisher.

• Beware of printing/publishing companies offering to design your book cover. They may overcharge, and design quality may be cookie cutter or amateur. They may also own the rights to the cover. You could end up owning the book's ISBN and text, but not the cover. If you are self-publishing, this may be a problem. If you are using a reputable traditional publisher, it is not. Your best bet as a self-publisher is to use a graphic designer recommended by seasoned self-published writers.

• Pay attention to qualifying language (such as "up to") in contracts. Also, it is generally best that a contract be time-limited. Note the scope of the contract. It should have clear borders. Insist on a "termination at will" clause in contracts. Make sure you understand the consequences of any "exclusive" language.

• Unless you've determined you are working with an established, reputable publisher, do not sign away the rights to your book, and don't give anyone an exclusive to print it or sell it. Consult a publication attorney if you have concerns about maintaining ownership.

PUBLISHING ELECTRONIC BOOKS: Electronic books are the wave of the future. In fact, some experts advise authors to skip the printed form and go directly to E-book sales channels. To get a book on an electronic platform, it must be reformatted and connected to an E-book vendor. There are companies that do this for a fee and/or a cut of earnings. These arrangements may lock you into a deal that limits options later. Review contracts carefully.

I've used CreateSpace to format books and connect them to Kindle. I've also done this formatting myself through Amazon's Kindle Direct Publishing (KDP), but it is tedious work. Neither CreateSpace nor Amazon will get you on all the major E-book devices, but those may not be your target markets anyway. No vendor is likely to have everything a self-publishing author needs. Multiple vendors may be required to meet broad marketing goals (a reason to avoid exclusive provisions in contracts). Many writers use *smashwords.com* to get books on multiple E-book platforms like Barnes and Noble's Nook and Sony Reader.

> **HINT: Some vanity publishers imply you must use their company to get on E-book sites. This is not true. You can**

do it yourself or use CreateSpace or some other vendor.

This wealth of detail about publishing might make you feel as though you've taken a drink from a fire hose. You may also feel your dream has been trampled and you must go back to watching reality television. Don't do that. File this information in the back of your mind, and pull it out when you need it. If you narrow your options to CreateSpace, Amazon, and Kindle as suggested in the model above, you won't need most of this information. Check out *createspace.com*.

LAUNCHING A PUBLISHING COMPANY: Starting a self-publishing company is intimidating, but once the setup work is done, you don't have to do it again. You've built the framework for future books. (If you have no plans to be a writer or to produce books other than a memoir, it is unlikely that taking this true self-publishing route is right for you.)

True indies form their own publishing company and keep everything in its name. You don't have to take this step if you are okay with a company doing registrations and being on record as the publisher. Many writers let CreateSpace or other companies do registrations for them (see Book Registrations below).

Publishing Company Name: Choose a name that looks good on a book. Don't send up flags that a book is self-published by using your author name for the publishing company or by selecting a name that doesn't sound businesslike. Using "publishing" in the name eliminates confusion on the book's spine as to what the name represents.

Check whether anyone has already registered the name nationally and, if not, register your company. This is done at the Federal website *business.gov.*

Register the publishing company name in your state as well. This may be referred to as a business license. It is usually done through the county clerk's office in conjunction with a sales tax application process. The registering organization should check to see if there is anyone already using that name in that state. If you don't use your legal name as the publishing company name, you may need to meet DBA (doing business as) registration requirements in your state. The county clerk's office and the Federal *business.gov* site have information on whom to contact in each state to determine registration and DBA requirements. Don't let these tedious details discourage you. You do them once, and you don't have to do them again. Just get them behind you.

BOOK REGISTRATIONS: To self-publish a book, you are required to do four things through the United States Government's contracted agency, R. R. Bowker.

-Register the publishing company.
-Obtain an ISBN identifier for each book.
-Obtain a bar code for each book.
-Register each book.

These actions are done online.

Registering the Publishing Company: After picking a name and registering it with state and federal entities, register it with Bowker. This is done at *bowker.com*.

ISBN: This is a unique **International Standard Book Number** that identifies a book and distinguishes it from others. The number is on the bar code on the back of books and on one of the first few pages of the book's text (referred to as *the publisher's page*). Libraries, bookstores, printers, customers, and others in the industry search for books with this number. ISBNs are available through Bowker.

Each ISBN represents a book. The cost will vary with how many you purchase. One costs $125. Ten can be purchased for $225. If you market both a printed copy and an E-book, some experts recommend getting a separate ISBN for each.

CreateSpace requires an ISBN before it will generate a proof copy (called galley copy in the industry). They will get one for you; however, when a vendor does this, they are listed as the publisher. This may or may not be important. I know writers who let CreateSpace get their ISBNs for them. I don't.

Bar Code: When the book's cover is designed, request from Bowker a bar code for the ISBN assigned to the book. This costs $35. Bar codes are used by libraries, bookstores, online sales companies, and distribution centers for reporting and inventory management. It's a high-resolution graphic in a TIFF or JPEG file sent electronically from Bowker. The bar code is placed in the lower right corner of the back of the book. Putting the price of the book on the bar code is optional. I used to do so but stopped because I adjust prices occasionally. You don't have to sell a book at the bar code price. (More about pricing in *Chapter 14 - Marketing and Distribution.*)

Registering a Book: This is done through Bowker when a book is ready for market. Registration puts the book on the national online *Books in Print Register* which provides a publishing company's contact information to the public. Search online for *myidentifiers.com*, click on the ISBN for the book to be registered, click on Edit ISBN and fill out all required data.

COPYRIGHTS: A copyright is a symbol of a serious publishing effort. Printing vendors and retail companies expect the copyright and the Library of Congress Control Number (LCCN) to be on the *publisher's page* of a book. However, it is not necessary to copyright a book to protect your rights. Once a book is printed, as of that date you have all rights to it unless you sign them away—something you normally don't want to do. In court, the print date typically takes precedence over the copyright date.

A copyright does not provide protection from someone taking your book and rewriting it. With different wording this is legal. This is one of the reasons some experts recommend sending only a couple of chapters when submitting manuscripts. (It is highly unlikely anyone is going to steal your memoir.)

To copyright a book, go to *copyright.gov*. This is a simple process and costs $35. Don't let anyone copyright the book for you without understanding the consequences. If you have concerns, consult a publishing attorney. You cannot copyright the title of a book, so books can have the same title. In those cases the ISBN, author name, and publishing company distinguish books from one another. You can check if a title has already been used.

HINT: Check book titles by searching *amazon.com, barnesandnoble.com,* and other book vendors.

LIBRARY OF CONGRESS: If you plan to sell to libraries, you must have a Library of Congress Card

Number (LCCN), also called a Preassigned Control Number (PCN). Other distribution channels may require it as well. If you self-publish, register this yourself so it is registered in your name. You do this at *loc.gov/publish/pcn*.

> **HINT: When going online to obtain registrations, make certain you're dealing directly with the agency. Companies put copycat websites on the internet to entice writers to do registrations through them for a fee. Writers don't realize they are working through an intermediary.**

PUBLICATION DISCLOSURES: On the back of the title page, include what is called the *publisher's page*, which provides the publisher information, copyright, ISBN, and LCCN. Include your website address. Study books and note the various formats and presentations. Some have lengthy disclaimers and legal jargon. It is your decision how much to invest in the legal implications. Believing nothing I write is important enough to attract legal attention, I forego the legal rhetoric.

CONTRACTS: Be cautious about signing contracts or agreements. They are structured to the advantage of the organization writing them. Read the fine print. Understand all terms and conditions. Highlight things you need to study. Google any terms you don't understand. (I received a printer's agreement so complicated I took the company off my prospect list.)

Be savvy when interpreting your percentage cuts. A 25% royalty might look good, but contract language that says your cut is a percent of "net" revenue as opposed to "retail" means the percentage is applied after discounts, publisher and agent cuts, overhead cost, and who knows what else. (You may never figure out the formula for determining overhead.) These can lower your portion substantially. Base any analysis on net dollars to you, not percentages. If you can't figure out what that is, avoid that company.

Publishing can be a challenge, and so can marketing. But don't give up. If you wrote a book, you can sure as heck sell it. If you are so inclined, make it your mission to create a book so interesting that people will pay to read it. Customize the marketing strategy to match your interests, goals, enthusiasm, and what works for you. The next chapter tells how to do that.

Chapter 14

MARKETING
AND DISTRIBUTION

The first rule of marketing is that you must have an exceptional book. Unless you have that, nothing you do will bring success in the marketplace. You must compete for readers with hundreds of thousands of ambitious, seasoned, skilled, and connected writers. If you are up for that, listen up.

Selling is a function far removed from the creative process of writing. To share a creation broadly, you must promote the heck out of it. Although some friends and family will buy your book, you'll be surprised how many expect you to give them one. You can't count on sales from those you know.

Companies will offer to market your book for a fee, usually a hefty one. They really can't do that effectively, although their sales pitch will suggest they can. You, as the author, must sell it. Even if you have an agent and a publisher, you still must sell. **When it comes to generating sales, you are *it*.**

MARKETING STRATEGIES: Here are four sales and distribution models for self-published authors:

> **Direct Sales:** The writer does selling and delivery. It can be done person-to-person or through the author's website. This approach yields the largest profit margin if printing costs are held down.

> **Vendor Online Sales:** This is the Amazon model. An expedient approach, it includes sales and fulfillment. It usually produces the most volume with the least amount of effort.

> **E-Books (electronic books):** This model is the most efficient. No printing or fulfillment is required. But readers expect lower prices so payout per book is low.

> **Retail Book Stores:** This approach is not typically viable for self-published authors.

DIRECT SALES: Under this scenario, the writer keeps an inventory of books and sells and distributes them. Personal contact through book signings, book club readings, speaking engagements, a website, and social media sites generates sales. For many writers, speaking engagements are the most lucrative.

HINT: Always be ready to sell. Have a few books in your car. Put them in a suitcase when you travel.

Under the direct-sell model, the author incurs printing and delivery costs and keeps an inventory of books on hand. No one takes a cut of the revenue.

HINT: In order to do direct selling when a vendor is also used to promote or sell, the author must maintain the right to print and sell himself in the contract with that vendor. Do not give anyone an exclusive right to print or sell. (As far as I know, Amazon's contracts allow writers to print and sell books themselves.)

Display your website in the book and on business cards, bookmarks, brochures, and social media sites.

HINT: Put contact and order details (email address, website) in the book. If you have more than one book, promote all of them in the back pages of each. With contact information, people can give feedback. Although reader feedback is rare, it is priceless. (I insert a bookmark in my books that tells how to post a

review on Amazon. Even with that information, very few people do so.)

WEBSITE SALES: A website can be used for direct sales or for vendor online sales (the Amazon model), depending on how it is set up. Here are two setup options.

(1) Direct Sales: You do sales, printing, and fulfillment. Link your website to *PayPal.* They take the order, collect the money, and email you where to send the book. You ship it from your inventory. *PayPal* withholds a small transaction fee and keeps a record of transactions. They periodically transfer your share of the money collected to your bank.

(2) Online Vendor: A simpler method is to link the website to Amazon or some other vendor and have them do sales, printing, and fulfillment. They take a cut for those services and deposit your share into your bank account. Most authors I know use this model.

HINT: Link your website to your Author Page on Amazon, and buyers will see a list of all your books.

To set up a website, you must:

(1) Buy the "Domain," (web address). It costs as little as $20 a year. You also need a vendor to connect your site to the web. *GoDaddy.com* is a popular one that does both domain and connection. Google "website domains" to find others.

HINT: Stay away from companies who put advertising you cannot control on the site. Read any agreements carefully.

The website address (name) you choose is important. Authors are "branded" through their name. Use your author name if it is not already taken. People are more likely to remember an author's name than the name of a self-publishing company.

(2) Design the Site: This is done through web-building software. You can do this yourself or hire someone to do it for you. Cost usually runs $1,000 to $2,000. If you use someone else, you may be dependent on them to make future changes. This can be costly and burdensome.

I paid GoDaddy $400 for training and used their web-building platform to design my site. I'm not technically astute, so this was frustrating at times, but it was also rewarding. I acquired a new skill set, and I can make changes myself. Some writers recommend *sandvox.com* or *wix.com* as writer-friendly, web-building sites.

A website is only a vehicle for selling. You cannot put it out there and expect sales to happen. No one knows it's there. **YOU must drive people to the site, and it must be a marketing marvel when they get there.**

SOCIAL MEDIA PROMOTION: Approach this medium thoughtfully, especially where personal relationships are involved. People don't appreciate frequent solicitation on social sites. You can easily overdo it. When a book is published, put the word out on social media, but don't mention it frequently. Find a way to be interesting through communications rather than being primarily focused on selling. What does your writing have to offer people?

Blogging provides an opportunity to interact with people and create a network of potential buyers. Publishers love writers who have a large blog following. Build followers requires giving readers useful/entertaining information so they will want more. Blogging offers an opportunity to share your voice, but don't count on it to deliver substantial sales.

There are social media experts who will design and execute a social marketing plan for a fee.

HINT: If you notice someone with impressive online advertisements, contact them and find out who is doing it for them.

As with other marketing arrangements, do a cost/benefit analysis on any proposals. Can you sell enough books and realize enough net profit to make the investment in marketing worthwhile?

Social media can require a huge investment of time, and in spite of the hype, few writers experience robust sales through these channels.

BOOK SIGNINGS: Book signings are a direct sell opportunity that can play a role in a writer's promotional portfolio. Odds are you won't be able to land a book signing at a chain like Barnes & Noble, but you can get one at a local bookstore. Signings may not yield substantial sales volumes, though, and they require considerable time and effort.

To do them right, you must send notices to newspapers and get on radio and television just ahead of the signing. This is doable. You may not nail a *Good Morning America* or *The Today Show* gig, but the prospects of getting on a local television or radio station are good.

I did several signings and never made much money. In fact, given signage, posters, table decorations, etc., I lost money. The most books I sold at such an event was twelve, and it took six hours to do it. This is not unusual. A popular bookstore told me the average books sold at a signing, even with publicity, was nine. Book signings are work.

HINT: Have a flyer to hand out with strong marketing content, a picture of the book's cover, and one of you as the author. Include contact information and details about other books you've written. Stand, rather than sit. Try to get a location at the front of the store or at another high-traffic area. (You are not a movie star. Customers will not come to you.) Offer every passerby a flyer, then invite them to take a peek at the book. Have comments prepared that persuade them they want to read it. (Notice I said, "read it," not "buy it.")

It is a stretch to expect person-to-person activities to generate substantial sales. This reflects the formidable prospect of reaching the 250-book average of self-published book sales, let alone exceeding it.

Even with this challenge, probably nothing you do has the potential to make you feel more like an author than a book signing. However, if you are intimidated about being on TV or radio and find book signings awkward or too much work, you have something in common with many writers, who tend to be an introverted bunch. Don't do signings if they take the joy out of the writing experience.

ONLINE SALES: How well your book sells and whether you make money on those sales depends on the quality and marketability of the book and the intensity of your efforts. To make a profit, you must execute a calculated marketing strategy at minimal cost. Amazon is the primary online sales channel at this time. It offers several approaches to selling, each with pluses and minuses. The cut Amazon takes varies by plan. Your book competes for sales with a massive volume of others. To get the best exposure, purchase a couple of books on selling online and study them. But remember this: Your ability to steer people to the site is the primary determiner of the level of sales success.

You can get lost in the shuffle of the huge mass of writers and books. If you put one of your key search words in on Amazon, your book may come up after thousands of others with the same key word (see Chapter 10 - *Producing a Cover*). Also, high sales volumes must be realized to offset printing and delivery costs and Amazon's cut. Be shrewd about picking a plan, setting a price, and working the marketing machine to the max.

HINT: Break it down. Do one thing each day toward selling. At the end of a month you'll have done thirty things.

I know writers who do all the things I've mentioned here and still don't make much. But they enjoy being authors and doing what authors do.

Being an author is not just about sales and money. There is prestige in being listed on the primary online retail book source in the world and being recognized as an author. Your book on Amazon does that for you.

MARKETING ELECTRONIC BOOKS: Some argue paper books are headed for the niche market. Although it is unlikely beloved printed books will go the way of the VHS tape, there is little doubt that there is an E-book explosion.

Optimal pricing strategies for electronic books are still evolving. Most E-book buyers are extremely price sensitive and books are priced substantially lower than the printed copy. Prices between $.99 and $9.99 are popular. I found my sweet spot at $2.99. This sounds low, but with E-books, there are no printing, inventory, or distribution costs. Also, I'm focused on sharing, not making money. I don't want to lose a sale because someone can't afford the book. (Some authors offer E-books free.) At these prices the profit margin is narrow.

Only with a good book, good luck, and fierce marketing can a writer sell enough to make money through this channel. The promise of the E-book market is alluring, though. If you are serious about marketing a book, designate a month to study up and give it a shot.

CHAIN BOOKSTORES: It might surprise you to learn this is not a lucrative market for most writers. National retail bookstores and stores like Walmart, Target, supermarkets, and airports rarely stock self-published books, and vanity books are generally shunned.

Although many writers see national bookstores as nirvana, there are severe negatives to doing business with them. They demand huge discounts and have an unattractive return book policy whereby books are returned to the publisher if they don't sell in a few weeks or months. A writer at a conference complained that a bookstore returned hundreds of her books with stickers on the front covers that could not be removed.

Purchasing protocol for these stores requires that they obtain books through wholesale distributors. Without the muscle of a major publisher, it's difficult to get into these stores. By comparison, online or electronic book channels are more attractive to most writers.

LOCAL BOOKSTORES: Although national bookstores may not take your book, local retail bookstores might buy a few or take them on consignment. They may even schedule a signing. Like all other sales channels, getting a book into a bookstore does not mean it will sell. You still have to steer people to the store to buy it.

OTHER RETAIL STORES: A memoir set in a geographical area might be of interest to gift shops, museums, cafes, and coffee houses in that vicinity.

LIBRARIES: Like national book chains, libraries, for the most part, have standard acquisition protocols through specific distributors. If your plan is to optimally apply your energy and time to channels with the most potential, libraries may not be a priority.

SALES PROMOTIONS: Schedule some kind of launch party near the publication date. Produce flyers, bookmarks, and business cards. Mail them to prospective buyers and insert them in books. Build a contact file, send emails, and make social media postings to announce when a book is published, how to order it, and details of the launch event.

> **HINT: Promote your book in October as a Christmas gift. In the spring, suggest it as a Mother's Day or Father's Day gift.**

You may invest considerable effort into sales promotions and still be challenged to beat the average self-published book sales figure of 250. Generating sales requires a full-court press of marketing techniques over an extended time. If you want to do that, study how to market books and dig in.

> **HINT: If you have the will, do everything to sell. If not, set marketing priorities. Test online and E-books channels through approaches that require minimum investment. If you have limited time and money, target methods that deliver the best results with the least effort and that you enjoy. Don't try to do everything.**

The reality might be that there is not a large market for your book. For memoirs, this is often the case.

That's okay if you define success as: You created it, put it out there, and those who read it enjoyed it.

PRICING: If you factor in all costs when pricing a book, you could price yourself out of the market. Books are selling for less in the current market, even in bookstores. After hiring an editor and cover designer, incurring print and delivery costs, paying business expenses, engaging technical support, and giving a printer and an online sales organization their cut, there will be little left for you. And those costs don't include the time you invested in writing the book. Only 5% of books published ever recover expenses. This is why making money on books is a tough goal.

Most books, whether in bookstores or online, are discounted by the retailer. You have no control over this. A book retail priced at $15.00 might be discounted to $7.99 or less. Most book buyers are price sensitive. Discounting is strategically smart, and most sellers do it.

You can print the price on the bar code or on the back of the book, or not. There is controversy over whether to do so. I don't do it because I adjust prices occasionally. The highest retail price you can set while still being competitive with other books is probably optimal, although there are those who advocate the lowest price possible. It's your call.

HINT: Check prices of comparable books in a bookstore and on Amazon before pricing your book.

A Federal Trade Commission (FTC) regulation requires that any deal made with one customer must be offered to all like customers at that time and through the same channel. The operative word here is "like." Different discounts for different categories of customers and different sales channels are allowed as are discounts based on volume.

FULFILLMENT/PRINT & DELIVER: When sales are direct to people, fulfillment is simple. They give the author money; he hands them a book. Sweet. When a writer receives orders through a website, mail, or email, he must distribute the books. This can be done by ordering a book from a POD vendor (like CreateSpace) and having them ship it to the buyer, or the writer can fulfill the order from his own inventory. The post office book rate (called media rate) to mail a book runs about $3.41 for a 280-page soft-back book. Bubble wrapped envelopes cost about $.75.

DEFINING MARKETING SUCCESS: Marketing is demanding. It is easy to get swept up in industry hype that defines success as volume of sales, but that is not for everyone. Consider opportunity costs—the money, time, and other activities you must give up in order to invest in marketing. You don't have to do it. You are successful as an author when a book is produced. You did it. It exists. It is out there for generations to come. Whether the book sells a little or a lot, it is shared.

Chapter 15

BUSINESS ISSUES

If you don't sell books, you don't have to deal with business issues, and none of the information in this chapter applies. When you cross over into selling them, you are essentially running a business and all that that implies.

BUSINESS OBJECTIVE: Decide whether you want to focus on writing for pleasure or for profit. Earnings may or may not be realized. The pleasure, on the other hand, is almost guaranteed. At any rate, consider what your goals are from a business perspective. They will drive many of your decisions.

BUSINESS STRUCTURE: When creating a publishing company or a business to sell books, keep it simple. A sole proprietorship is the simplest structure. You might want to use that form unless there is a compelling reason to do otherwise. Consult an accountant or lawyer if you need advice on structure and liability risks.

BANK ACCOUNT: For tax purposes it's important to keep personal and business transactions separate. Open a business bank account in your publishing company's name and run all transactions (income and expense) through that account. Buyers often make checks out to the publishing company. Without an account in that name, you'll have trouble cashing/ depositing them. (Checks made out in your name, on the other hand, can be deposited into the business account with no problem since you are the signatory.)

CREDIT CARD: A business credit card keeps business charges separate from personal ones and simplifies accounting and tax preparation.

BUSINESS CONTACT POINTS: You can set up separate phone, P.O. Box, and email contact points in the publishing company or your business name. Whether you do that or not depends on how serious you are about keeping business and personal transactions separate as well as your sensitivity to privacy.

ACCOUNTING: You might not make a profit, but if you have revenue, you must track it and costs and report them for tax purposes. Most likely the costs will exceed the revenue and you won't owe income tax. You can probably take a loss for three years or so. At some point, though, the IRS and state tax commissions expect a business to show a profit. They may seek to disallow losses on the premise that the business is unlikely to ever yield a profit and is a hobby. When you reach this point, you can still deduct costs up to the amount of revenue, even if you can no longer take the loss. A tax expert can guide you through the tax maze.

> **HINT: Factor the impact of taxes and other business expenses into any calculations when projecting net money earned or lost on books.**

BUSINESS TAXES (SALES TAX): Whether realizing a profit or not, if you sell books, you are required to pay local city or county sales taxes, sometimes called transaction or business taxes. In many states you pay none if your book sells through the web or to someone out of state; however, this situation is fluid. States are passing laws to capture that tax revenue.

Register your business with the local tax commission or franchise board, most likely at the county court house, and comply with any business tax requirements. They will assign a permit number which identifies your company.

FEDERAL EIN: Businesses are required to have a Federal Employer Identification Number (EIN). You can get one free at *irs.gov/ein*. That name is a misnomer because you must have one whether you have any employees or not. It is IRS form SS-4. Anyone who sends you money may require the EIN in order to report to the IRS money disbursed to you. Some state tax commissions require the EIN as well.

At this point, you may feel overwhelmed. When the business requirements of self-publishing hit me and I discovered all I had to manage in order to sell books, it was too much and I gave up. I wanted to write books, not run a business. However, over time, these things got done, step by step.

One month you build a website, the next month you hook it into PayPal or Amazon. Next you register your business, get an EIN, and open a business bank account. Every week you accomplish another business task. A few months later, the business is in full swing, the steep learning curve is behind you, everything is set up, and you are off and running.

Don't let business tasks kill your dream. Once many of them are done, you don't have to do them again. You have built the base. Time spent on setup is an investment which pays off over and over in the future. You are in business.

Chapter 16

A LIFE CAPTURED

There is an immense reservoir of wisdom out there which few people recognize and even fewer tap in to—the wealth of experience from lives fully lived. When a life is gone, precious treasures of a uniquely magnificent story are lost forever unless captured in some manner. Writing that story is a generous, expressive way to create something tangible and enduring—a life story. This is no little thing.

Many life stories are not written because people mistakenly believe they cannot write. The primary goal of this book is to dispel that notion. Its purpose is to provide tools and perspectives that give people confidence they can turn their life or someone else's into a unique, relevant, and beautiful story.

It's important throughout the creative and often tedious process of producing a memoir, or any other book, that writers understand why they are doing it. The objective should always be at the forefront.

If you become integrated into the writing community while doing this project, you will be inundated with ideas on how to sell books and make money. This is because most serious writers are focused on that. Stay focused on the creative process and know why you write.

Don't listen to what others say you want versus what you really want. Don't listen to what others tell you will make you happy versus what will make you happy. And don't listen to what others tell you is possible versus what is reality. And, most important, define success on your own terms. If defined as everyone loving and buying your book, you may be disappointed. If defined as creating it and sharing it, success is inevitable. In memoir, a writer is sharing a life and leaving a legacy. That *is* success. You can feel good about doing that.

To ensure you enjoy the process, consider a flexible, fluid timeframe for accomplishing all that is required to make the memoir happen. Set soft dates rather than hard ones and liberally adjust timelines as necessary to avoid stress. Take things step by step.

> Break the process down. Embrace tasks in increments of weeks or months. Over time, significant progress is inevitable.

When overwhelmed, focus on what has been accomplished, not what must be done. Relish the process and revel in the personal growth it produces. Then explore what amazing progress can be accomplished in the next month, and the next, and the next.

As this book demonstrates, there are nuances to producing a captivating life story. To the novice memoir writer, this means there is a lot to learn. Don't let learning or anything else delay getting started with the actual capturing of the story, though. Write, interview key players, dig for details, and make notes. Make these activities a priority. Life is fleeting. Avoid the regret of delay. Allow yourself to do some shabby writing in the moment. The polish can come later.

Also, don't wait until the memoir is finished to share it. Share printed copies of chapters with others. The delight a person experiences when they realize someone cared enough to write about them is sweet. It makes them feel relevant. It should make you feel so as well. And don't wait to finish the memoir so you can include "the final chapter" of a person's life. Put it out there. You can add their final days later in an epilogue. If the memoir is about you, tie it up in a bow and finish it off even though there is more life to come. Enjoy the fruits of your efforts. And while you're at it, enjoy being a writer.

While at a writers' conference in New York City, I sat in a diner at two o'clock in the morning after a marathon night of writing. A dazed young woman wearing Christmas lights as a necklace and two young men sat in the booth next to me. The girl's head occasionally dangled perilously close to her catsup-covered french fries. She lamented to her male companions that her boyfriend would be furious with her for getting so wasted.

One of the young men comforted her by suggesting, "It'll be all right. He'll get over it." To prove his point, he said, "I threw up on my girlfriend once, and she's still my girlfriend."

Now, that was a writer's dream observation—a jewel. This is an excerpt from what I wrote about it. (The full story is in the Appendix - *Technique 3 - Tidbits*) Seek out the jewels in your life and write about them.

A sense of purpose will fuel the determination and persistence required to produce a captivating memoir. My wish for you is that you find a reason for capturing a life story—one that carries you through the tasks. I wish for you that you enjoy the process and revel in its results. I wish for you that you create a memoir so crazy wonderful that when someone finds it in an attic generations from now, they hold it in their hands and say out loud: "Wow!"

APPENDIX

MEMOIR ACTION PLAN

This list of action steps may be intimidating, but some won't apply to you and the actions can be spread over several years. Do a few steps each month. Keep in mind what the life story you create will mean to others. Remember, you are creating legacy.

—GETTING STARTED—

____**Write, Interview, Collect Information.**

____**Define Purpose, Vision, Frame of Reference, and Tone.** Why are you writing a life story? What do you want to accomplish? How do you see it affecting others? What does it mean to you?

____**Identify Audience.** Who are they and what do you want them to think and feel when they read the story?

____**Define Success.** Do you aspire to simply create something and share it with whomever is interested, or to become a writer by profession? Does success mean being a publisher and a business person? Is it important to you to sell large volumes and make money to feel successful?

____**Determine Strategy.** Are you going to take the simple route of writing, printing, and distributing the memoir, or are you going to go all out and publish and sell it?

____**Develop a Learning Plan.** Take writing courses. Attend seminars and conferences. Read books about writing and publishing. Research author blogs online. Join a writers' group.

_____**Interview People.** Inquire about events, personalities, connections, and daily life. Look for tidbits and hooks. Probe. Focus on the feelings around events. Verify dates, facts, and details.

_____**Collect Photos.**

_____**Take Professional "Author" Picture for Cover.**

_____**Set Up a Place to Write.**

_____**Set Up a Place in Which to Drop Reminder Notes.**

_____**Join a Writers Group.**

_____**Seek Out a Critique Group.**

—WRITING—

_____**Create First Draft.** Regurgitate. Get it all out. Create a comprehensive first draft (not to be published). Dedicate months to this, if necessary. Save the draft in both electronic file and hard copy form.

_____**Copy First Draft to a Working File.** This is the file used to develop the manuscript of the book.

_____**Set Up Outtakes File.** Writing taken out of the working file goes into this file for possible use later.

_____**Review Working Draft.** Move to the outtakes file any narrative that does not make it into the final memoir. You might want it later (target approximately 300 pages or around 80,000 words).

____**Identify Themes.** Identify and understand the major themes of a life—the perspectives that drove choices.

____**Organize text**. Develop a draft *table of contents*. Use it to move text into logical locations in the manuscript. Revise table as book evolves. Determine section breaks, chapter titles, and subtitles.

____**Establish Structure.** Organize beginning, middle, and end. The beginning says what the book is about. The ending tells how things turned out. The first paragraph of a chapter tells what that chapter is about. The last paragraph transitions to the next chapter. String stories together. Balance intensity, action, and humor throughout the book to avoid weak chapters.

____**Determine a Narrative Arc.** (Google: *narrative arc).*

____**Determine a Character Arc** (Google: *character arc*). Show how characters change over time—how they evolve.

____**Develop a Strong First Paragraph.**

Do Run-Throughs:
   ___**Develop characters.** In-depth and sympathetic.
   ___**Describe environment.** Background, settings, scenes, weather, culture, details of the times.
   ___**Build out stories.** Write story by story. Use layering, tidbits, defining moments, rebel jewels.
   ___**Interject historical events.** Tie personal experiences to historical incidents.

___**Make minor events major ones.** Round out incidents with detail and perspective. Shape them into colorful tales.

___**Add dialogue and quotes.**

___**Add sentiment.** Paint a picture of feelings and passions as well as connections with people, animals, and nature. Interject perspectives of others (how they view the world).

___**Apply reader perspective.** Remove self-indulgent comments and write for the reader. Don't try to show off and look smart.

___**Introduce humor.** Add humor and repeat humorous themes throughout the manuscript.

___**Repeat references to key life events.** Show how these create impact throughout life.

___**Tighten up wording.** Don't state the obvious. Remove unnecessary words and redundant sentences, paragraphs, or even chapters.

___**Create transitions.** Improve flow from word to word, sentence to sentence, paragraph to paragraph, and chapter to chapter.

___**Thread.** Run threads of life's themes throughout book. Repeat key points. (Don't overdo.) Tie back and tie forward.

___**Write in active voice where possible.**

___**Find opportunities to *show* instead of *tell*.**

___**Assure consistent *point of view*.** No head-hopping.

___**Remove/replace pronouns.** Eliminate *I, me, you,* and *your* where appropriate.

___**Enhance word selection.** Replace trite, boring words with more interesting, colorful, and descriptive ones. Use a thesaurus.

___**Replace or remove weak words.**

___**Evaluate every sentence.** Focus on structure and effectiveness of words and phrases. Put strongest sentences at the beginning and end of paragraphs.

___**Ensure all sentences and paragraphs have relevance.** Each one entertaining, touching, interesting, conveying a lesson learned, moving the story forward, or contributing to it in some way. Eliminate redundancies.

___**Emphasize words.** Make sure to use the right words. Put important words at end of sentences to make them stronger. Use italics, bolding, quotation marks, but do so cautiously (don't overdo).

___**Enhance format.** Add white space, break up paragraphs, indent paragraphs, and create lists.

___**Take a break.** Let the manuscript bake.

___**Read out loud.** Concentrate on flow, transitions, sequences, and story continuity. Resolve awkward wording. Seek rhythm.

___**Review spelling, punctuation, grammar.** Question suspect words, review punctuation marks for appropriateness and consistency, check for grammar errors.

___**Read from the perspective of others.**

___**Read while pretending to be your worst critic.**

___**Edit.** Proof several times and then have someone else proof—a fresh set of eyes.

___**Share drafts.** Seek feedback.

___**Read for fun.**

___**Repeat any run-throughs as needed.**

—MECHANICS—

___**Establish Computer Backup Capabilities.** Check occasionally to make sure working (calendar dates to check).

213

____**Develop Technical Skills.** Take courses. Learn formatting, graphic design layout, file transmission, and web building or recruit someone to do these things.

____**Format Text.** Establish book size, set margins, spacing, font sizes and letter styles, headers/footers, page numbering system, chapter breaks and headings.

____**Develop Photo Insertion Skills.** Collect photos. Scan and digitally load, adjust/enhance, assure 300 DPI resolution where possible, add captions, inline into text.

____**Develop Proofreading/Editing Skills.** Study proofreading techniques. Engage another person to proof.

____**Establish Source for Grammar/Punctuation Rules.** Select style book source and an online search engine.

____**Establish Source for Spelling Rules and Word Use.** (Spell Check, search engine, thesaurus, and dictionary.)

—COVER—

____**Layout/Graphic Design.** Recruit a friend or relative with technical design experience, or find a professional source, or learn to do it yourself.

____**Determine Title, Subtitle, Hooks.** Use bold, artful fonts.

____**Design Cover (Front, Spine, and Back).** Use layout software for producing cover unless putting in a notebook.

____**Determine Cover Content.** Seek input from someone with a marketing background.

____**Insert Author Photo and Three-Sentence Biography.**

____**Consider Seeking Reviews.** Define process.

____**Proof.** Have another set of eyes proof the cover.

—PRINTING—

____**Study Printing Industry**. Understand traditional, and vanity publishing as well as print on demand (POD). Learn how to avoid scammers. Do cost/benefit analysis on offerings.

____**Determine Marketing/Distribution Model and Choose Sales Channel (if going to sell).** Printer selection may depend on whether intention is to sell (see *Marketing).*

____**Identify Prospective Printers.** Check them out on *writersbeware.com.*

____**Review Printing Contracts in Detail.** Don't agree to give up rights. Don't give anyone *an exclusive* to print or market. Don't use a printer who insists on putting their logo on your book (if you are self-publishing).

____**Select Printer.**

____**Determine Printer File Transmission Requirements** (typically PDF format).

____**Submit Files.** Send text and cover files.

____**Order Galley Copies for Proofing and Reviews.**

____**Review Proof, Make Changes and Corrections.**

____**Resubmit Text and Cover Files.**

____**Determine Volume and Order a Supply of Books.** Order only as many as needed at the time.

____**Prepare for Shipment Delivery/Storage.**

****

If you do not intend to sell the memoir and are simply producing it for friends and family, many of the following action steps do not apply.

****

—SELF-PUBLISHING—

____**Determine Publishing Strategy.** Study publishing business. Avoid scammers and opportunists. Consider cost benefit of alternatives. Reassess: Do you want to publish and sell? Why? Have clear objectives.

____**Name Your Publishing Company.** Check state and national registries to determine if already used.

____**Register Name with Federal Agency.** *business.gov*
____**Register Name with State Agency.** *business.gov*
____**Register Company** with *Bowker.com*
____**Purchase ISBN** at *Bowker.com*

_____**Decide Price of Book.** Decide if price put on bar code.

_____**Purchase Bar Code** from Bowker. *myidentifiers.com*

_____**Register Book** with Bowker. *myidentifiers.com*

_____**Copyright Book.** Use national copyright office, *copyright.gov*. Don't let anyone else do this for you.

_____**Obtain Library of Congress Number (LCCN).** *loc.gov/publish/pcn*

_____**When Complete, Send Copy to Library of Congress.** (I suspect few writers meet this requirement.)

_____**Develop and Execute E-book Strategy.**

—MARKETING AND DISTRIBUTION—

_____**Study Book Marketing.** Read books, study online sources, review writers' blogs, and research sales options.

_____**Investigate Marketing Services.** Before contracting for any marketing services, do a cost/benefit analysis and check vendors out on *writersbeware.com*.

_____**Determine Marketing Strategy.**

_____**Develop Direct Sales Plan.**

_____**Assess Online and E-book Opportunities.**

_____**Develop Promotions.** Flyers, contact lists, social media, bookmarks, business cards, inserts.

_____**Develop Website.**

_____**Install Payment Process for Website.** PayPal or link to Amazon or some other payment source.

_____**Arrange for Signings and Media Promotions.**

_____**Contact Book Clubs and Writers' Groups.**

____**Publicize.** Contact friends and relatives. Use social media. Promote book as gifts.

—SET UP BUSINESS—

____**Engage Accountant.**
____**Determine Business Structure.**
____**Set Up Bookkeeping Processes.**
____**Set Up Business Contact Points.** PO Box, business email and phone (all optional).
____**Open a Business Bank Account.**
____**Obtain Business Credit Card.**
____**Meet County/State Requirements.** Business license, sales tax registration, DBA (doing business as) filing. Each state is different.
____**Obtain Federal EIN.** Employer Identification Number (needed for tax purposes). *irs.gov/ein*
____**Set Up Sales Tax Payment Capability.**
____**Calendar Business Requirements/Tax File Dates.**

—CELEBRATE—

____**Throw Launch Party to Celebrate Book.**

Note: Writers often ask how long all this will take. If you are not working and can commit the time, it may take two to three years. Don't rush. Take whatever time you need and enjoy the process. It will fill up your life. **If people who have never written a book wonder why it is taking so long to write the memoir, show them this action plan.**

EXAMPLES OF
FIVE WRITING TECHNIQUES

(Excerpts From *Out of Iowa—Into Oklahoma, Red Heels and Smokin'*, and *Hey, Kids, Watch This*)

Technique 1 - Break it Down
Write Story by Story

My next running amuck experience occurred when I took a road trip to California with Donna Mae, who was moving there. . . . Her dog, Toby, made the trip interesting because it was too hot to leave him in the car. We had to eat all our meals at drive-throughs. Then there was the fact that he had to pee. No grass could be found when we stopped for gas in the Mojave Desert. I placed him down among the cacti to do his business. He danced around frantically on the hot sand, so I picked him up and held him a few inches above ground. I shook him gently to induce him to pee, which he had not done since Flagstaff, Arizona. He was way overdue. Toby looked back at me like: "What the hell are you doing?" I finally gave up and tossed him in the car, telling Donna Mae, "We need to get out of here pronto. We must find grass." My tone was desperate. She gave me a strange look until I explained Toby's dilemma.

Toby is temperamental. Perhaps that is an understatement. When I'm unable to reach Donna Mae by phone, I worry Toby has eaten her. She walked him late one night on our trip. This concerned me, although not enough to miss my favorite television show. So I didn't accompany her. She left the hotel room to walk an overenthusiastic Toby as I nestled in the comfort of my bed to watch television. I asked her, "If you don't come back, can I have your car?" (*Out of Iowa—Into Oklahoma*)

Technique 2 - Apply Layers
Start with Facts and Layer on Details and Feelings

. . . The crisis rallied my folks to my side. They spent time in Oklahoma supporting me after realizing if they didn't, they could lose me. It was a scary and puzzling time for them. I recall sitting on the sofa beside Mom and crying so hard she rocked me. She held me and rocked me. I finally slept with my head in her lap, her stroking my hair. I felt like a child. How difficult that must have been for her. (Thirty years later, she would do this again.) . . .

I was afraid and exhausted from fighting a raging battle all day every day. I tried so hard to make it on my own in the midst of threats and challenges. My therapist suggested I give up the fight. "Give up," he said, "Just lean into it. Flow with it." Giving up was a strange concept to me. I had children and responsibilities. But he persuaded me to chill and let things play out. He was right. I coped better.

I let go and began taking things as they came rather than trying to solve all the problems in my world. This was an important lesson. I've used this "give up the fight" approach to coping many times since. I've shared it with others who were in crisis mode. Sometimes we just try too hard. . .

I moved into a one-day-at-a-time existence while keeping my eye on becoming independent and providing for my family. It had been all about survival, but gradually, I began thinking about a serious career and "a good life" for my children. I began to think about the prospect of life being fun. (*Out Of Iowa—Into Oklahoma*)

Technique 3 - Mine Tidbits
Embellish the Details

As Grandma Go Go, I have my limits when it comes to child rearing. I get overwhelmed easily, particularly when there is more than one toddler involved. You know you have too many whelms when Cheerios from breakfast and peas from lunch are left on the floor as a later snack for a foraging toddler, when it becomes okay that a child is wearing something backward or wrong side out, when you give up on snapping every other snap on toddler clothing and don't snap any at all, when you have given up plucking your eyebrows, when shaving legs is not even on the radar, when it doesn't occur to you to make your bed even if company is coming, when you are taking morning vitamins at bedtime if at all, and when it becomes irrelevant that you are wearing clothing backward or wrong side out. . . .

While simultaneously playing an alphabet game and trains with my three-year-old sidekick (we were multi-tasking), I had an out-of-body experience. I floated around the room observing myself saying: "Come on over here little *s*. Big *R* you need to scoot over there." Meanwhile, a train circled on a track near my butt. This play activity occurred after running toy cars through a car wash, hiding in a cardboard box that smelled like, well, like cardboard, performing a chemistry experiment with Fruit Loops, and singing several choruses of a song about sitting in a high chair banging a spoon. It was pure, unmitigated craziness. And I loved it, which proved I had lost my mind; therefore, the out-of-body experience.

The revelation was not over yet. My floating-around-the-room self began answering questions from my on-the-carpet-in-the-middle-of-a-train-track self. The question was: "Is this a big *W* or a big *M?*" Later, while pondering letters *d* and *b*, my out-of-body self realized I was in a loop while my other self was busy responding to a squeaky voice complaining my butt was on the track blocking Thomas the Train. I had too many whelms—definitely. (*Out of Iowa— Into Oklahoma*)

At a writers' conference in New York City, I took a break from an all-night writing marathon. An Oklahoma woman out of my element, I sat in a diner at two a.m. drinking coffee.

The Friday night crowd trailed in after a frenzied night of fun. Some patrons were decked out in nightclub garb. In contrast, I looked like a French cafe slouch in clothes comfortable enough to be classified as pajamas and hair resembling a cat toy. I was not bothered by my appearance, though. In New York City, nothing is peculiar.

One might wonder why a sixty-something woman from Tulsa, Oklahoma, graced this setting. I was a writer, and serious writers at one time or another make a pilgrimage of sorts to New York. This quest for two a.m. coffee created a bonus adventure for this tourist who stumbled upon a flavor of the city's night life. Writers are thieves, and I decided to observe the action for the purpose of stealing ideas for a future composition. Prospects were abundant.

Exposed young girls with vocabularies embellished with the words "like" and "whatever" and blustery, cocky young men with shaved heads and baggy pants slung low enough to reveal underwear coexisted splendidly after a Friday night of partying. The women paraded by—wobbling in four-inch heels—as young men in the next booth delivered the common pickup line of the testosterone-fueled night animals, "Oh my god! You are so beautiful. Oh my god!" They didn't say this to me, of course. I was still trying to lose baby fat from my firstborn child forty-eight years ago.

These comments were directed at rumpled, smudged-up, glassy-eyed unfortunates in skirts so short it appeared they had put on blouses and forgotten their skirts. One girl's dress was hiked up so high the crotch of her thong was visible in the front and her bare ass in the back. Although this visual was an assault on my mind (I thought, *Gawd*), the guys were so taken by *thong girl* they pounded the table. Unable to contain themselves, the young men rose from their seats as if their butts were filled with helium. Following her, they omitted the "You are so beautiful," and just said, "Oh my god! Oh my god! Oh my god!"

A few gang-like fellows were so rambunctious I expected someone would throw them out. Wondering where to hide if they started shooting, I knocked on the partition around my booth to determine if a bullet could pass through it and evaluated the prospect of squeezing myself under the table if necessary. Then I realized a good part of the crowd behaved this way, and it was normal, at least at that hour and in that setting. No matter what happened, no one paid any attention.

So I abandoned the concerned tourist role and settled in for a session of discreet observation. I did, however, make a mental note. *The next time I come to New York I will explore the prospect of a more sophisticated hotel, one that leaves chocolates on my pillow and whose guests drink Grand Marnier at two in the morning.*

I hung around longer than intended because my waiter, the swiper, periodically passed by at the speed of light, swooping up my half-filled coffee cup for refills. Since I'd dosed it with the required daily supplement of fiber, I had to drink each successive cup to ensure I got my thirty grams. Once accomplished, I left with a severe caffeine buzz, but not before overhearing a confounding conversation in the next booth.

A dazed young woman wearing Christmas lights as a necklace, whose head occasionally dangled perilously close to her catsup-covered french fries, lamented to her male companions that her boyfriend would be furious with her for getting so wasted. One of them comforted her by suggesting, "It'll be all right. He'll get over it." To prove his point he said, "I threw up on my girlfriend once, and she's still my girlfriend."

There I was, a mature woman from Tulsa, Oklahoma, embracing my passion and drinking coffee with the night children of New York City. In spite of their joyful exuberance, which contrasted glaringly with my mellow, pajama-clad, fiber-seeking persona, I had no envy of them. I was relevant and vital. I was a writer—a fresh label for me, a new identity I embraced with passion. This passion gave me purpose and helped me get my moxie back. Through it I found bliss. Through it I served. (*Red Heels and Smokin'—How I Got My Moxie Back*)

Technique 4 - Discover Defining Moments
Write About What Changed Everything

For some years, Mel [my daughter] and her sophisticated, jet-setting friends flew all over the place for business and fun—New York to take a company public and ring the bell at the stock exchange, Louisville for the Kentucky Derby, Tampa for New Year's, Vegas for Halloween, and Trinidad for Carnival, etc. Then, in her mid-thirties, motherhood happened, which changed everything. She is now settled in California with a family and our shopping strategy has shifted. We used to doll up and shop and lunch at marvelous places. Now we shop separately while one of us is home with toddlers. Or we divide and conquer, each of us taking a child. We don't dress up nice anymore. I usually look like a bag lady with a human appendage. My shopping venue is the nearest dollar store where the objective is finding the diaper aisle and locating a toy lawn mower while managing a toddler who does not want to move past the gum machine. As for dining in marvelous places, that ain't happening unless Chuck E. Cheese qualifies. It is a sad, sad, sorry situation. (*Out of Iowa—Into Oklahoma*)

Mom never accepted the fact that medicine could not fix everything. Determined to fix her hearing problem, she asked her doctor at every visit, "What is wrong with my ears?" He had heard this question so many times, that in frustration one day he responded, "YOU CAN'T HEAR." An eye doctor also told her she couldn't see. Soon she was unable to walk, and that changed everything. Sadly, she sat around waiting for the next thing she couldn't do. . . .

We used to go someplace every day. We were *Thelma and Louise,* heading out on some small adventure. But the days of adventures were soon behind us. I could tell she was declining. Medical crises gained momentum. I tried to prepare her mentally for the impending nursing home stage of her life, but as is often the case, she had difficulty accepting the inevitable.

Mom went into a nursing home at eighty-eight. . . .I watched her struggle with the reality of her situation. She said, "I can't walk so good, can't hear so good, can't see so good, and I am no good." She did have some vitality left, though, as evidenced by her being in trouble with the staff for speeding in her wheelchair. . . . (*Out of Iowa—Into Oklahoma*)

Technique 5 - Expose Rebel Jewels
Include Rascal Behavior and Bold Departures

It was scary to watch him [my son] stock car race. I sat in the stands nestled among his fans. During warmup laps, when he passed in front of us, he gave us the "thumb up."

Everyone hooted and hollered. I would say: "He's so cute," which tickled his friends. Although anxious before a race, once one started, I could get into it. . . The deathly quiet in the stands after a wreck where he was knocked senseless paralyzed me. His fans ran to the fence, but I could not move. Eventually, the "thumb up" came out of his car window. The announcer raved, the crowd roared, and I could breathe again.

Marty was always a fearless risk taker, which I find both fascinating and terrifying. A fireworks aficionado, he put on shows every Fourth of July. He once rappelled down a high rise building for a charity event. I watch his antics when I can, going to drag races, stock car races, pool tournaments, or whatever, always recognizing that it is his world, and I am just visiting. There were times when I was more a part of his world than I bargained for.

I dropped my car off at his shop for him to do work on it. He gave me a loaner. Little did I know it was one of his drag racing cars—revved up, rocking, and ready to roll. I sat at the end of the driveway, waiting for a break in traffic so I could pull out. When I got it, I pressed the pedal and peeled out, fishtailing all over the place. *Wow!* However, I still had not grasped the magnitude of the situation.

Idling at a red light down the street, I noticed how loud the vehicle was. Chug, chug, chugging away—and bouncing. The frigging car was bouncing. I glanced over at a man in the lane next to me who was clearly amazed an old woman was driving this hot rod. He smiled and revved his engine. Then my car died. I mean it just coughed it up and frigging died. I started it back up, turned around, and headed back to the shop. When I walked in, Marty and his friends rolled with laughter. "Hey, Mom, if you need more power, there's nitrous in the trunk." Humor at my expense was common among them, and I played my role, pitched a conniption fit, and left with a suitable car. (*Out of Iowa—Into Oklahoma*)

I make certain my pharmacist remembers me as a person, not a prescription. When I pick up medication, I ask questions: "Will this change the color of my eyes or interact with Jamba Juice? Are projectile vomiting and anal leakage side effects? What are the odds of involuntary movements occurring, and will they be permanent? Do you think the seat warmer in my car caused my yeast infection?"

When pills are a different shape and color, I complain to the pharmacist, "I'm concerned these are male hormones and I'll grow a mustache."

I occasionally tell him, "I don't care what everyone else says, I like you anyway." As a result of all this, my pharmacist knows who I am.

I also ask my doctor important questions like, "What happens if I eat expired yogurt?" I once suggested transvaginal ultrasound would be a good name for a rock band. I requested Demerol because my feet were getting bigger and something weird happened to my earlobes. When he referred me to a radiologist, I asked if the guy could fix my radio. My doctor knows who I am. (*Hey, Kids, Watch This—Go BEYOND Aging Well*)

The Craft of Writing
Polish and Shine

In the genre of memoir, it is more important to write something than to write it perfectly. (A flawed manuscript has a certain charm.) It's your call on the extent that craft is embraced. Don't let the challenges of craft take away your joy of writing. If you are so inclined, you can polish a story by using the computer "find" capability to search for opportunities for improvement. Below are *find and fix* possibilities. It would be a major task to search all of them. Be aware of them and focus on what works for you.

Avoid the Following Words Where Possible. THEY ARE NOT "WRONG." They are in every book, including this one, but are often overused, unnecessary, or trite. Most are out of favor with writing experts, agents, and publishers because they cry out for a better word. Consider rewriting to avoid them.

That, The, Now, Very, Really, Truly, Still, Yet, Then, Suddenly, Actually, Certainly, Nearly, Probably, Clearly, Rather, Somewhat, Well, So, Must, Just, Any, Got, Quite, A little, A lot, Some, All, Maybe, Perhaps, Literally, Almost, Kind of, Sort of, Pretty, Pretty Much, The Fact Is, As A Matter of Fact

Had, Has, Would, Could - (possible tense or strength issues: "Dad *would* stoke the fire." vs "Dad stoked the fire.")

It, There, This, They, Thing(s), Something, Item - These are *empty* or *dummy words*. Use more descriptive ones where possible.

Basically, Totally, and the vernacular **Like** - Don't use these words, even in conversation—unless you're at a rave concert in California.

Like - When used in simile, *like* is a good word, but don't overuse. Alternatives are: *as, as though, as if,* and *similar to*. (Note: Using too many **similes** or **metaphors** weakens their impact.)

Tried To, Started To, Began To - Get down to what is happening. Example: "She cried." instead of "She began to cry."

Adverbs - Use sparingly. Most verbs are stronger on their own. Search for words ending in "ly" and reconsider them.

Never, Always, or Every - Use only when the word is literally true.

Feel, Felt, Seems, Noticed, Looked, Saw, Heard, Knew, Learned, Thought, Realized, Hoped, Wondered, Guessed - You may be *Telling* when *Showing* is better (Google: *Show* vs *Tell*)

Be, Being, By, Been, Was, Were, Is - May mean *passive voice* instead of *active voice*. Possible rewrite. (Google: *Passive vs Active Voice*)

"ing" - Using too many words ending in "ing" is not good craft. Beginning a sentence with an "ing" word is okay occasionally to vary sentence structure, but don't do too often.

I, My, Me, Myself - Used too often is distracting. Rewrite to eliminate where possible. Grammar: *I, my,* and *me* are last when used with another person. *Me* vs *My* or Myself is tricky. (Google for rules)

That, This, Which, Who:
> *That* vs *This* is determined by proximity (Caution: *This* might imply present tense.)
> *That* vs *Which* (Clue: *Which* is preceded by a comma.)
> *That* vs *Who* - Use *who* when referring to people (not *that).*

Who vs Whom - Use *whom* when it is the object of a preposition unless it sounds hopelessly awkward, which it sometimes does. Otherwise, mentally re-word a sentence. If *him* sounds right, use *whom*. If *he* sounds right, use *who*. (Some consider *whom* too formal since people rarely use it in speech.)

If vs Whether - There are sticky nuances here. (Google: *If* vs *Whether*)

Can vs May - *Can* = ability / *May* = permission (When speaking, who cares which is used? When writing, it matters.)

All Ready = fully prepared. / **Already** = previously. / **Alright** is not a word. Use **All Right**.

Awhile vs A While - a*while* = adverb / *a while* = a period of time (Insert "for" in front of *awhile*. If it works, use *a while*.)

Around = In the area of / **Round** = shape or not exact number. Don't use **A Round** unless you are talking about ammunition.

Lay(s), Laid, Laying = set *object/something* down
Lie(s), Lay(s), Laying, Lain = a *person* rests or reclines. (Don't use *laid* for a person, normally.)

Affect vs Effect - *Affect* = verb / *Effect* = noun (usually) (Google: *Affect* vs *Effect*)

i.e. vs e.g. - *i.e.* = *that is* / *e.g.* = *for example.* There is controversy over use and punctuation. A good alternative: Just say "That is" or "For example"

Onto vs On To - O*nto* = upon / Otherwise use O*n To*

In To vs Into - *In To* = adverb / *Into* = preposition expressing motion

It's vs Its - *It's* is a contractions for *It Is. Its* shows possession. (Consider replacing *It* with a more descriptive word.)

You're vs Your - *You're* is a contraction for *you are. Your* shows possession.

They're = they are / **Their** = possession / **There** = place (Consider replacing these with more descriptive words.)

There Is vs There Are - The verb *is* or *are* is determined by whether the object of that verb is singular or plural.

Who's vs Whose/Chose vs Choose/Lead vs Led/Whether vs Weather/Met vs Meant - Words commonly used incorrectly.

Backward(s) - Backward is American, Backwards is English. Same for Afterward(s). Neither is wrong. Be consistent.

But, And, So, Yet, Or - Coordinating conjunctions (comma precedes them) connect two sentences, **each with a noun and a verb**. Use economically to avoid long, "run-on" sentences. Consider breaking into separate sentences. (It's generally accepted to start a sentence with these words, but don't overdo.)

Word Choice - Use the right word. Examples: *Convince* = of something vs *Persuade* = do something (followed by *to*). *Fewer* = number (countable) vs *Less* = measurement, time, distance. (Check dictionary)

Sentence Structure - Vary throughout a paragraph. (Starting every sentence with a noun is boring.)

Paragraph Structure - Place most important sentences at the beginning and ending of paragraphs.

Transitions - Assure flow between sentences, paragraphs, chapters.

Key Words - Avoid using important words twice in a paragraph. Use exceptionally unique words and phrases only two or three times in a book, unless they are part of the theme. (Don't overdo book's theme.)

Active vs Passive Voice - *Passive voice* is **not wrong,** but *active voice* is stronger. ***Passive***: The house was painted by Al. ***Active***: Al painted the house. Look for passive verbs (*be, by being, been, was, were, is*). Consider a rewrite.(Google: *Active* vs *Passive*)

Person - *I, My, Me, We, Us, Our, Ours / You, Your, Yours / He, Him, His, She, Her, Hers, They, Them, Their:* Check for consistency of *person*. Some shifts are appropriate, but in general, consistency is best. Most memoirs and auto-biographies are written in first person/past tense and biographies in third person. (Google: *first, second, third person.*)

Tense - Present: *Are, Is, Have, Has, Do, Does.* **Past:** *Was, Were, Had, Did, Done.* Check for consistency of tense. (Google: *present/past/past perfect tense.*) Variations in tense are appropriate—even necessary—but should be intentional and not jolt or confuse readers. (Note: *Was* is used when the subject is singular, w*ere* when plural, except when a *condition* is involved: "*If* he *were* to go.")

Point of View - Be consistent within chapters/scenes about whose POV you are writing from. No "head-hopping" unless done for strategic reasons. Identify POV in first few sentences of each chapter or scene. (Google: *Point of View*)

Dialogue Attribute - Put the *he said/she said* after the quote. Don't use fancy words in an attribute (Google: *dialogue technique*).

Commas - Don't use a comma before *that, because, as, since, or as well.* Do use a comma before *such as* and none after. Use a comma before *which* and words ending in *ing* (usually). Use a comma after introductory prepositional phrases. Don't use a comma when only month and year (June 2016).

A Series Separated by Commas - If possible, put the shortest phrase first and longest one last (perhaps making the last one a zinger). Phrasing of each item in a series should be compatible (called *parallel phrasing*—Google it). Leaving out the *Oxford comma* (final comma in a series—before the *and* or *or*) was popular; however, this is trending back. **Use the Oxford comma.**

Quotation Marks and Punctuation - Periods and commas are **always** on the inside of quotation marks. Question marks and exclamation marks may be inside or outside depending on whether they are part of the quote. Only rarely is an exclamation mark appropriate. Most experts say to use **only** to show excessive excitement or shouting.

Dash - Avoid using two hyphens for a dash. Not wrong, but implies "amateur." Use *em dash* (—). (Google: *hyphen/en/em dash*) Most computers have a function to generate *em dash*. (On *Apple*, when Times New Roman used, it is: hold *option* while hitting two *hyphens*.) *Em dash* is used instead of commas for emphasis, to indicate an interruption, or to suggest "more to come" (when at end of a paragraph).

Ellipses (. . .) - Indicates an omission, usually from a quote. Should be a space before (except when after a quote) and after.

Spacing - Use only one space after periods and colons.

Recommended books on writing:

Stephen King - *On Writing*
William Zinsser - *On Writing Well*
Anne Lamott - *Bird by Bird*

Recommended reference books:

Strunk and White - *The Elements of Style* (pocket size)
Susan Thurman - *The Only Grammar Book You'll Ever Need*

How to shine:

-Proofreading/Editing: Make an editor your wingman. Get a good one and learn from proposed edits.

-Deliver a Strong Beginning and End

-Create A Memorable Title. Examples:

Poem: *Mom* could be: *I've Been Mom-ed*

Essay: *On Aging* could be: *The Inconvenience of Being Old*

Blog: *Eating Disorders* could be: *An Adversarial Relationship with Donuts*

-Use Compelling, Intriguing, Appropriate Words:

Instead of *home*, consider *hovel, cottage, mansion, bungalow, pad, crib*

Instead of *little*, consider *petite, lithe, willowy, dainty, diminutive, elfin*

Instead of *big*, consider *Amazonian, massive, towering, enormous, colossal*

Instead of *find out*, consider *discover, uncover, explore, fathom, unearth*

With a good noun, you don't need an adjective.
With a powerful verb, you don't need an adverb.

-Use Words in Unusual Ways: Example: Use *feral* to describe children on spring break in Florida or love gone wrong. Use *eccentric* to describe a chair or pickup truck.

-Use Colorful Details and Brilliant Descriptions:

Describe wine as *articulate* or as *prancing grapes*

Describe memories as *keen, raw, cruel, delightful, fuzzy, poignant,* or *haunting*

Describe a bushy beard as *overachieving*

Describe a buffet as a *luau of desserts*

-Avoid Clichés. They are trite. Use your own wonderful words.

NOTE: These craft recommendations don't always mean alternatives are wrong. Rules are controversial among experts. **Also, there are reasons to break rules.** Writers often violate them in the interest of style and practicality. In general, though, complying with rules of craft is a gift to readers, and it is important to agents and publishers. When they observe a lack of craft in the first few pages of a manuscript, they will move on to more expert writers. **Don't let a struggle with craft overwhelm you, take away your joy of writing, or override your goal to write a memoir. Sharing a life story trumps craft.**

Books By Nikki Hanna

Available on Amazon, Kindle, and www.nikkihanna.com

OUT OF IOWA—INTO OKLAHOMA
You Can Take the Girl Out of Iowa, but
You Can't Take the Iowa Out of the Girl

Laced with witticisms and lessons learned, Hanna's memoir delivers an inspirational romp through the challenges of being exposed to diverse cultures. Stories of struggles and triumphs experienced while growing up on an Iowa farm, moving to Oklahoma, and becoming a successful urban business executive show how she navigated the traumas of change. Readers will laugh, cry, and fall in love with the colorful characters in her world. Hanna's wit and resourceful interpretation of her past delivers an honest, clever, and often ridiculously entertaining life story.

CAPTURE LIFE
Write a Memoir

Brimming with inspiration and advice, this book introduces writing techniques that encourage even the most reticent person to write. Clever writing techniques and processes prove that anyone can create an enticing life story—and self-publish it. Hanna guides writers through the minefield of printing and publishing with simple, inexpensive strategies. She serves up wise and helpful counsel peppered with tools, checklists, and examples of life stories designed to inform and entertain. Both seasoned and novice writers will benefit from this book.

LEADERSHIP SAVVY
How to Stand Out as a Leader

Fresh, relevant, and practical advice in this book for both aspiring and experienced leaders demonstrates how to be an exceptional influence, how to promote employee loyalty, and how to build an energized work force. Based on over forty years of business experience in corporate America, Hanna defines leadership as "service to those you lead." She identifies Ten Common Leadership Mistakes, Ten Management Myths, and Five Keys to Career Success. Her proven and often novel approaches to leadership deliver results and give readers a competitive edge. Leaders will stand out. And their companies, associates, employees, and customers will benefit.

RED HEELS AND SMOKIN'
How I Got My Moxie Back

If you think being sixty-something is a bummer, humorist Nikki Hanna will convince you otherwise. A playful and inspiring tale of the adventures of a woman who redefined aging, *Red Heels and Smokin'* describes the transitional years of the author's life after retirement. A gutsy, zany, and sometimes outrageous woman, Hanna is bold and brutally candid as she dishes out interpretations of her passage into the third trimester of life. By resurrecting the moxie that served her well in younger years, she turns a tsunami of crises that threaten to overwhelm her into an amusing story of hope and passion. Hanna's thoughtful and sometimes outrageous interpretations of her aging experience deliver generous doses of wisdom, common sense, surprises, hope, and entertainment. Her story will have readers rooting for her rally and perhaps strategizing to initiate one of their own.

HEY, KIDS, WATCH THIS
Go BEYOND Aging Well

The central message of this intelligent, perceptive book about aging is that regardless of how old you are, you can be a person in crescendo. And you can do this no matter what happens. Hanna shows how a person creates legacy through how they view themselves as an older person and how they live their third trimester of life. She encourages readers to find purpose in softening the lives of others. Hanna addresses hard issue head on but takes the edge off them with a clever format and jaunty tales spiked with humor and quirky characters. *Hey, Kids, Watch This* is a delightful and inspiring read for older people and those who care about them.

ABOUT THE AUTHOR
www.nikkihanna.com

When asked to describe herself in one sentence, Nikki Hanna said, "I'm a metropolitan gal who never quite reached the level of refinement and sophistication that label implies." The contradictions reflected in this description are the basis of her humorous prose. She has a BS Degree in Business Education and Journalism and an MBA from The University of Tulsa. A retired CPA and Toastmaster, Hanna has years of experience in management and as an executive for one of the country's largest companies. She also served as a consultant on national industry task forces, as a board member for corporations, and as an advisor on curriculum development and strategic planning for educational institutions and charity organizations.

Hanna describes her writing as irreverent, quirky humor with strong messages. As an author, writing coach, teacher, and writing contest judge, she is dedicated to inspiring others. She speaks on the craft of writing, memoir writing, and finding joy and purpose in writing as well as on aging, leadership, and women's issues.

In addition to numerous awards for poetry, essays, books, and short stories, Hanna received the Oklahoma Writers' Federation's *Crème de la Crème* Award and the Rose State College Outstanding Writer Award. Book awards include the National Indie Excellence Award, the USA Best Book Finalist Award, and two international Book Excellence Awards. Her books are available on Amazon/Kindle and through her website.

Hanna lives in Tulsa, Oklahoma. Her children think she has become a bit of a pistol in her old age. They tell her, "Don't call me if you get thrown in jail." Four grandchildren consider her the toy fairy, and those in California believe she lives at the airport.

Hanna is available for customized workshops as well as for speeches, entertainment programs, readings, and coaching novice writers. Comments on books are welcome at: neqhanna@sbcglobal.net

44141235R00134

Made in the USA
San Bernardino, CA
07 January 2017